THE RULE OF LAW
IDEAL OR IDEOLOGY

Edited by

Allan C. Hutchinson
LL.B.(Hons.),LL.M.
BARRISTER OF GRAY'S INN

Patrick Monahan
B.A.,M.A.,LL.B.,LL.M.
MEMBER OF THE ONTARIO BAR

CARSWELL
Toronto • Calgary • Vancouver
1987

Canadian Cataloguing in Publication Data
Main entry under title:

The Rule of law

ISBN 0-459-39540-8

1. Rule of law. I. Hutchinson, Allan C.
II. Monahan, Patrick.

K3171.R84   1987   340'.11   C87–093409–0

73491

Preface

This collection of essays had its beginning in a conference held at Osgoode Hall Law School, York University, Toronto, in April 1984. We thank the Social Sciences and Humanities Research Council of Canada for its generous financial support of that event. We are also very grateful to Josh Moon, Susan Sills and Penny Spence for their dedication and hard work. Without their important contribution, the conference would not have been a success.

We owe a special debt of gratitude to our friend Dean John McCamus. Throughout, he has been a valued source of encouragement, counsel and reassurance. At the risk of embarrassment, we dedicate this book to him.

Preface

Contributors

ALLAN HUTCHINSON and PATRICK MONAHAN are law professors at Osgoode Hall Law School of York University, Toronto. Their published work has focused on law and political theory. Hutchinson has a forthcoming book, entitled *Dwelling on the Threshold: Critical Essays on Modern Legal Thought* and Monahan on *Politics and the Constitution: The Charter, Federalism and the Courts.*

DUNCAN KENNEDY is professor of law at Harvard Law School. He is a founding member of the Critical Legal Studies Movement and he has published extensively on radical legal theory and legal education. His most recent publication is *Legal Education as Training for Hierarchy: A Polemic Against the System* (1984).

THEODORE LOWI is the John L. Senior Professor of American Institutions at Cornell University. He has published numerous books on American government, including *The End of Liberalism* (2nd ed., 1979) and *The Politics of Disorder* (1971).

PHILIPPE NONET is professor of law and sociology at the University of California, Berkeley. His books include *Administrative Justice* (1970) and *Law and Society in Transition* (1978).

MICHAEL SANDEL is professor of government at Harvard University. A political philosopher, his most recent writings are *Liberalism and the Limits of Justice* (1983) and *Liberalism and its Critics* (1984).

JUDITH SHKLAR is the John Cowles Professor of Government at Harvard University. Her writings span a vast range of topics. Among her publications are *Legalism* (2nd ed., 1986) and *Ordinary Virtues* (1984).

ERNEST WEINRIB is professor of law and classics at the University of Toronto. He has published widely in legal theory and is presently completing a book entitled *The Natural Law of Torts.*

Contents

Introduction

The Rule of Law is a rare and protean principle of our political tradition. Unlike other ideals, it has withstood the ravages of constitutional time and remains a contemporary clarion-call to political justice. Apparently transcending partisan concerns, it is embraced and venerated by virtually all shades of political opinion. The Rule of Law's central core comprises the enduring values of regularity and restraint, embodied in the slogan of "a government of laws, not men." Its very generality is the reason for its durability and contestability. Interpreted and appropriated by seemingly contradictory groups, it is the will-o'-the-wisp of political history. Although the central jewel in liberalism's crown, its universal appeal is attested to by E.P. Thompson's invocation of it from the political left as an "unqualified human good".

Notwithstanding its transcendent and long-standing popularity, the Rule of Law has been under mounting pressure in modern society. In both popular and elite circles, commitment to this ideal can no longer be assumed. Against a backdrop of lawlessness and social frustration, certain *causes célèbres* reveal the extent of popular disaffection with the legal and established order. The continuing drama involving Dr. Henry Morgentaler is a case in point. Over the past decade, he has continually and openly defied legal limitations on the availability of abortions, having been acquitted by juries in two provinces in the face of clear legal prohibition. Interestingly, both critics and supporters of these verdicts invoked the authority of the Rule of Law. While the critics claimed that such actions jeopardized the whole administration of justice, others maintained that the jury constituted a necessary safety valve for the justice system. Far from quelling the controversy, the legal machinations have fueled the intensity of opposition and disagreement. Both sides have taken the struggle to the streets. In the process, the legal system itself has become a focus for dissent.

Such trends and outbursts are not merely Canadian phenomena. In England, along with similar demonstrations of political protest, the unsuccessful prosecution of Clive Ponting points up the estrangement of state legality from popular sentiment. Ponting had revealed to a Member of Parliament classified information contradicting the government's account of the British sinking of the Argentinian 'Belgrano' in the Falklands war. Although conceding that he had broken the law, Ponting was acquitted by a jury which followed public conscience over almost irresistible "legal" argument. Similar issues surfaced in America in the Bernhard Goetz affair, the so-called subway vigilante. After shooting four youths who accosted him, Goetz generated a massive and spontaneous groundswell of popular support. Initially proclaimed by many as a heroic figure, his act was seen as a symbol of populist frustration with an impotent criminal justice bureaucracy. Although short-lived, the source of his celebrity and sympathy was his defiance of the basic principles of legality.

Once the preserve of radical youth and its assault on "the system," civil disobedience has become a political strategy for both left and right. Bernhard Goetz has joined Abby Hoffman on the streets of the city, if on different sides of the road. Popular activism cuts across traditional political categories and is pursued by environmentalists, farmers groups, doctors, nuclear protestors and both sides of the bitter abortion dispute.

While issues of law and legality have always been central to liberal-democratic theory, these popular events have given an urgency and freshness to such theorizing. The Rule of Law has become an item of high priority on the agenda of political and legal theory. This concern has been particularly acute in Canada, with the enactment of the Charter of Rights and Freedoms, whose preamble tells us that "Canada is founded upon principles that recognize the supremacy of God and the rule of law." Judges and lawyers find themselves in the eye of the political storm, struggling with issues as diverse and divisive as cruise missile testing, mandatory retirement and Sunday closing laws. Courts have been charged with performing the invidious task of reconciling the interests of the individual with those of the community; this enterprise has concerned and confounded polities since the dawn of political theory. The Charter symbolizes the judicialization of the political and the corresponding politicalization of the judicial.

The ambition of this timely collection of essays is to capture the flavour and fullness of the contemporary debate over the Rule of Law. As the title of the book suggests, *The Rule of Law: Ideal or Ideology?*, the aim is neither to defend the Rule of Law nor to pillory it. It is hoped to deepen and enrich our understanding of the Rule of Law, to take stock of its present predicament and to evaluate its significance and future prospects. The contributors approach the subject from a variety of disciplinary perspectives and political standpoints.

Despite the range and diversity of opinion, the essays fall into three groups. The first group consists of essays by Judith Shklar, Theodore Lowi and Ernest Weinrib. Although lamenting the Rule of Law's present performance, they believe that it can be revitalized within the confines of traditional liberal theory and practice. In her essay, "Political Theory and the Rule of Law", Shklar argues that there are two distinct archetypes of the Rule of Law, attributable to the work of Aristotle and Montesquieu. However, the distinction has become blurred and the two ideals incoherent. The political purposes and settings which gave them significance have been forgotten and the Rule of Law is now situated in an intellectual and political vacuum. Critically surveying the work of such theorists as Friedrich von Hayek, Ronald Dworkin and Roberto Unger, she argues cogently that the Rule of Law should be recognized as an essential element of constitutional government generally and of representative democracy in particular. Its boundaries are set by enduring concerns over the fear of violence, the insecurities of arbitrary government and the discriminations of injustice. By returning to these elemental concerns, Shklar maintains that the Rule of Law might reclaim its importance in political theory and practice.

Theodore Lowi's essay, "The Welfare State, The New Regulation and The Rule of Law", begins with the observation that traditional values associated with the Rule of Law are virtually non-existent in the state regulation of the 1970s and 1980s. Administrative agencies operate under vague grants of discretion without meaningful rules or standards to guide their activities. In an erudite account, Lowi links the decline of the Rule of Law to more pervasive cultural trends: the decline of notions of personal responsibility, "systems thinking" and the bureaucratization of authority. Despite the proliferation of "interest groups", there is no longer a constituency to support the Rule of Law. Nevertheless, he refuses to write off the Rule of Law. Even if it is no longer possible to formulate meaningful standards in legislation, Lowi believes that we can still study the retreat with care rather than simply "capitulate into the merciful arms of the administrative state."

Ernest Weinrib, in his essay "The Intelligibility of the Rule of Law", observes a paradox: the Rule of Law is typically contrasted to rule by individuals, yet it must always depend on the acts of particular individuals for its creation and administration. Given the inescapable role of human agency, Weinrib asks whether the Rule of Law is intelligible as an ideal. In his affirmative response, he seeks to demonstrate the possibility of a non-instrumental conception of law. This conception insulates the ideal of law itself from the particular purposes which might be periodically projected onto it by political and economic interest. Weinrib's elegant analysis focuses on private law, arguing that this body of law embodies Aristotle's notion of corrective justice since it concerns itself with immediate transactions between parties as opposed to any general criterion of distributive justice. He maintains that the particular features of corrective justice yield form, content and thus intelligibility to private law.

The second group of essays, by Michael Sandel and ourselves, attack the individualistic foundations of liberal theory and its use of the Rule of Law to stymie communal values. In his essay "The Political Theory of the Procedural Republic", Sandel reasserts the republican tradition against the present dominance of liberal rights-based theories. He attempts to expose the fragility of any liberal defence based on moral relativism, demonstrating the callous instrumentality of utilitarianism and the illusory neutrality of a rights-based ethic. Sandel sets the republican virtues of community and citizenship against the moral vacuity of liberal individualism. Suggesting their different practical recommendations, he shows how the monolithic tendencies of Rule of Law thinking overwhelm local forms of communal life. Charting the three historical phases in the transition from the republican to the liberal constitutional order, Sandel argues that, in contemporary America, liberty stands in opposition to democracy. People are "more entangled, but less attached, than ever before." The Rule of Law has been appropriated by liberals in their misconceived ambition to supplant the republican tradition.

In our essay "Democracy and the Rule of Law", we attack recent attempts to characterize the Rule of Law as the butler of democracy. Judicial review has been falsely celebrated as the triumph of detached philosophical deliberation over heated political haggling. After tracing the historical and theoretical connections between the Rule of Law and liberal democracy, we condemn the elite and marginal practice of constitutional adjudication. Reasserting the primacy of democratic and communal values over legalistic and individualistic ones, we seek to sketch a practical vision of rigorous democratic politics, in which the Rule of Law would occupy a much more humble position.

The final two essays by Philippe Nonet and Duncan Kennedy highlight the importance of differentiating the internal from the external perspective in experiencing and understanding the Rule of Law. In his essay "Is That the Rule That Was?", Nonet brings to the discussion a continental flavour and engages in some metaphysical, but pertinent musings on the Rule of Law. He reports on a (hypothetical?) dialogue with his

Californian law students at the end of his annual series of lectures. He reflects on how, why and what he ought to respond to his students' deceptively innocent question, "Is that still the Rule in this land?" Nonet's ethical dilemma centres on whether he should accept the philosophically profound distinction between theory and practice, doing and thinking, acting and observing: should he answer by achieving some external vantage point from which to survey the legal system or should he assume an internal attitude towards the legal enterprise? Whatever the anthropological or historical 'truth', he concludes that his responsibility *as a teacher of law* is to persuade his students that "law is an art learned by practice." The Rule of Law does not inhabit some rationalistic universe nor can it withstand rigorous intellectual scrutiny; it has to be experienced and lived. The moral of Nonet's homily is topical and to the point: the Rule of Law is a maxim of political action and not a precept of ethical reflection. Only by such a commitment can American citizens and lawyers "wrench American law out of its futurity, make it a presence, and begin to build a past to which they can later look with pride."

Duncan Kennedy continues the experiential approach to the Rule of Law but from a more radical perspective. In his accessible, if dauntingly entitled essay, "Toward a Critical Phenomenology of Judging", Kennedy tries to get inside the mind of the judge and understand the way he or she experiences "the law". In so doing, he hopes to evoke and describe how law operates as a constitutive social force. He imagines himself as a District Court Judge deciding a labour dispute and enquires how free or constrained he would be when there is an apparent conflict between "the law" and how he wants the case to come out. As a leading figure in the controversial "Critical Legal Studies Movement", Kennedy challenges the existence and authority of any professional knowledge of the Rule of Law. For him, the "experienced objectivity" of legal rules is both real and contingent; "rule application is something that does happen, but it is *never* something that *has* to happen." The implication of Kennedy's critical assault on legal objectivity is to expose the value-laden and potentially radical character of the judicial role.

Whatever their considerable differences, the contributors to this volume are unified by their belief in the enduring importance of the Rule of Law as a central artifact in our legal and political culture. Indeed, it is noteworthy that the Rule of Law remains a topical focus of contemporary debate fully one hundred years after the publication of Dicey's seminal work on the question. Perhaps it is the essence of the debate that it can never be finally resolved, but only provisionally advanced. This need not be a cause of dismay but an impetus for reinvigorating our commit-

ment to those aspects of the Rule of Law worth preserving. Paul Brest
has captured the challenge:

> Examining the "Rule of Law"—even at the risk of discovering that it is entirely
> illusory—is a necessary step toward a society that can satisfy the aspirations that
> make us hold to the concept so tenaciously.

Allan C. Hutchinson and Patrick Monahan

Political Theory and The Rule of Law

Judith N. Shklar

It would not be very difficult to show that the phrase "the Rule of Law" has become meaningless thanks to ideological abuse and general over-use. It may well have become just another one of those self-congratulatory rhetorical devices that grace the public utterances of Anglo-American politicians. No intellectual effort need therefore be wasted on this bit of ruling–class chatter. There is much to be said for this view of the matter. From the perspective of an historian it is, however, irrelevant. The Rule of Law did, after all, have a very significant place in the vocabulary of political theory once, so important in fact that it may well be worth recalling. Moreover, since legal theorists still invoke and argue about it, there may also be some point in comparing its present intellectual status with its original meaning. This may turn out to be not only an exercise in recollection, but also a diagnostic experiment. In the following pages I shall try to show that there are two quite distinct archetypes of the Rule of Law and that these have become blurred by now and reduced to incoherence because the political purposes and settings that gave them their significance have been forgotten. With some interpretive licence I shall attribute the two models to Aristotle and Montesquieu respectively. Then I shall suggest that contemporary theories fail because they have lost a sense of what the political objectives of the ideal of the Rule of Law originally were and have come up with no plausible restatement. The upshot is that the Rule of Law is now situated, intellectually, in a political vacuum.

The Rule of Law originally had two quite distinct meanings. It referred either to an entire way of life, or merely to several specific public institutions. The first of these models can be attributed to Aristotle, who presented the Rule of Law as nothing less than the rule of reason. The second version sees the Rule of Law as those institutional restraints that prevent governmental agents from oppressing the rest of society. Aristotle's Rule of Law has an enormous ethical and intellectual scope, but it applies to only very few persons in the polity. Montesquieu's account is of a limited number of protective arrangements which are, however, meant to benefit every member of the society, though only in a few of their mutual relations. It is not the reign of reason, but it is the spirit of the criminal law of a free people. Aristotle's Rule of Law is, in fact, perfectly compatible not only with the slave society of ancient Athens, but with the modern "dual state". Such a state may have a perfectly fair and principled private law system, and also a harsh, erratic criminal control system, but it is a "dual state" because some of its population is simply declared to be subhuman, and a public danger, and as such excluded from the legal order entirely. They are part of a second state, run usually by different agents of the government, but with the full approval of those who staff the "first" of the two states. Such was the government of the United States until the Civil War and in some ways thereafter. Such also was Nazi Germany and such is South Africa today. I mention only these states because they are part of "the Western tradition", and are included in its legal development. There are no remnants of a Byzantine past to confuse the historical picture here.

In contrast to Aristotle's rule of reason, Montesquieu's Rule of Law is designed to stand in stark contrast not only to simple "oriental" despotism but also to the dual state with which he was well-acquainted, as his remarks on modern slavery show. If it is to avoid these conditions, the Rule of Law must take certain types of human conduct entirely out of public control, because they cannot be regulated or prevented without physical cruelty, arbitrariness and the creation of unremitting fear in the population. Coercive government must resort to an excess of violence when it attempts to effectively control religious belief and practice, consensual sex and expressions of public opinion. The Rule of Law is meant to put a fence around the innocent citizen so that she may feel secure in these and all other legal activities. That implies that public officials will be hampered by judicial agents from interfering in these volatile and intensely personal forms of conduct. The judicial magistracy will, moreover, impose rigid self-restraints upon itself which will also enhance the sense of personal security of the citizenry. They will fear the office of the law, not its administrators. Commerce, unlike religion, was not among the areas immune to governmental control. That is because Montesquieu's justification for limited government was grounded in a psychology, not in a theory of public efficiency or natural rights. His view of limited government could be called the rule to control criminal law. Contemporary legal theory still relies quite heavily on these two original models, but they have tended to ignore every political reality outside the courtroom or hurled the notion of ruling into such abstraction that it appears to occur in no recognizable context.

In Aristotle's account the single most important condition for the Rule of Law is the character one must impute to those who make legal judgments. Justice is the constant disposition to act fairly and lawfully, not merely the occasional performance of such actions. It is part of such a character to reason syllogistically and to do so his passions must be silent. In the course of forensic argument distorted syllogisms will of course be urged upon those who must judge. That indeed is in the nature of persuasive reasoning, but those who judge, be they few or many, must go beyond it to reason their way to a logically necessary conclusion. To achieve that they must understand exactly just how forensic rhetoric and persuasive reasoning work, while their own ratiocination is free from irrational imperfections. For that a settled ethical character is as necessary as is intelligence itself.

The benefit to society of judgments made by men of such character is considerable. Without such justice no one is secure in his material possessions and even in his social values. Moreover, in the structure of politics the presence of men with such a mind-set, most usually middle-class moderates, has the effect of inhibiting the self-destructive proclivities that tend to afflict most regimes. The rule of reason depends decidedly on the capacity of the sane to persuade others to practise some degree of self restraint and to maintain the legal order that best fits the ethical structure of a polity. To have a stable system of restraining rules would seem to put enormous burdens on just men in their daily conduct. They are required, in addition to their ratiocinating and political skills, to possess the psychological ability to recognize the claims of others as if these were their own. The just man sees the merits and deserts of others exactly as if he himself were making a claim on those grounds. He draws no difference between himself and another or between two other opposed claimants. He can see all the demands of others and his own on a perfectly equal footing. When he is asked to decide a dispute or punish a wrong he sticks as closely to the rules as possible, because that is how he would want to be treated as a litigant. His task is simply to restore the previous balance and no irrelevancy may disturb his determinations. Without Aristotle's confidence in syllogistic reasoning this picture of perfect judgment would not make sense, nor would its claim to rationality stand. It is, however, part of a very powerful psychology as well. The powers of reasoning are part of the whole mentality of a man who has the capacity and inclination to see all claims impartially. That is not only required for judges, but of anyone who engages in fair exchanges, but it is clear that the supremely just activity on which everyone in society depends is epitomized by judging in courts of law. For it is there that justice is activated into legality. The rationality of this procedure is made especially plausible since it is a form of social control that applies to only a very limited part of the population and then to only some human relationships. Women and slaves are not governed by the norms of either justice or law. These people like children are part of a domestic economy that is ordered on more personal lines. Moreover, there are relations of friendship and magnanimity which may involve other aspects of the best male character than its justice, which does not distinguish between friend and foe. The point that seems to me to matter most for Aristotle's understanding of the Rule of Law, is its concentration on the judging agent, the dispenser of legal justice, the man or men of reason and of syllogism put to work in the arena where everyone else is driven by physical or political appetite. On their shoulders rests the responsibility for preserving the basic standards of the polity in their daily application, and for maintaining reasonable modes of discourse in the political arena. The picture is one of mediation, far more than of social control with all its uncertainties. Control is left to the masters of the domestic sphere.[1]

For an altogether different picture of the Rule of Law one cannot do better than to look at Montesquieu's version. While Aristotle's Rule of Law as reason served several vital political purposes, Montesquieu's really has only one aim, to protect the ruled against the aggression of those who rule. While it embraces all people, it fulfils only one fundamental aim, freedom from fear, which, to be sure was for Montesquieu supremely important. Its range is thus far narrower than Aristotle's Rule of Law, but it applies to far more people, to everyone to be precise. To realize the objectives of this kind of Rule of Law does not require any exceptional degree of virtue. The English, among whom Montesquieu saw it flourish, were far from admirable in many respects in his view. All that was needed for the Rule of Law in Europe, given its many fortunate historical and geographic circumstances, was a properly equilibrated political system in which power was checked by power in such a way that neither the violent urges of kings, nor the arbitrariness of legislatures could impinge directly upon the individual in such a way as to frighten her and make her feel insecure in her daily life. With religious opinion, consensual sex among adults and the public expression of public opinions decriminalized, the only task of the judiciary was to condemn

---

1 See especially *Nichomachean Ethics*, Book V, *Rhetoric*, Book I, ss. 1366b–1370a, 1373b–1377b and *Politics*, Book III, ss. 1285b–1287b and Book IV, ss. 1295a–1296b.

the guilty of legally known crimes defined as acts threatening the security of others, and to protect the innocent accused of such acts. Procedure in criminal cases is what this Rule of Law is all about. That is what makes the imperative of the independence of the judiciary also comprehensible. The idea is not so much to ensure judicial rectitude and public confidence, as to prevent the executive and its many agents from imposing their powers, interests, and persecutive inclinations upon the judiciary. The magistrate can then be perceived as the citizen's most necessary, and also most likely, protector. This whole scheme is ultimately based on a very basic dichotomy. The ultimate spiritual and political struggle is always between war and law. Rome chose war and lost everything. If France were to choose world monarchy and war instead of the English path to liberty and law, it too would be doomed to a deadly despotism. That is the fate that the Rule of Law, as the principle of legality in criminal cases fortified by a multitude of procedural safeguards, was capable of averting. It is very much "made", indeed, planned law. For all his respect for mores and customs, "inspired" rather than invented, as instruments of social control, Montesquieu was far too aware of the need for conscious political action to trust history to take care of Europe. He knew that judicial systems did not grow. They serve known purposes and are chosen and defended.[2]

This version of the Rule of Law is evidently quite compatible with a strong theory of individual rights. Indeed, in America that was to be the case. It is not, however, in the first instance a theory of rights. The institutions of judicial citizen protection may create rights, but they exist in order to avoid what Montesquieu took to be the greatest of human evils, constant fear created by the threats of violence and the actual cruelties of the holders of military power in society. The Rule of Law is the one way ruling classes have of imposing controls upon each other. Even so passionate a critic of the English ruling classes of the 18th century as E.P. Thompson, after all, agrees with him on that point. England was not a gulag society and its political classes had to some degree shackled themselves.[3] That is what was then meant by the Rule of Law.

The most influential restatement of the Rule of Law since the 18th century has been Dicey's unfortunate outburst of Anglo-Saxon parochialism. In his version the Rule of Law was both traditionalized and formalized. Not entirely without encouragement from Montesquieu, but wildly exaggerated, he began by finding the Rule of Law in-

---

2 *De l'Esprit des Lois*, Chs., VI, XI, ss. 3, 4, 6, 18, 19; XIX, ss. 12, 14, 16; XXVI, s. 20.
3 E.P. Thompson, *Whigs and Hunters* (London, 1975), pp. 258–269.

herent in the remote English past, in the depth of the early middle ages. Its validity rested on its antiquity, on its having grown, rather than being badly made, as was the case among the unfortunate countries of the Continent, especially France and Belgium. Its second pillar was that all cases were judged by the same body of men, following a single body of rules. The judges of the common law courts had slowly developed a suitable system, so that England had escaped that threat to liberty, administrative law, in which legally qualified tribunals dealt specifically with cases involving civil servants. Of the criminal law only habeas corpus mattered to Dicey, but the political arrangements of the English constitution did concern him. They were part of the Rule of Law. The Rule of Law was thus both trivialized as the peculiar patrimony of one and only one national order, and formalized, by the insistance that only one set of inherited procedures and court practices could sustain it. Not the structure or purposes of juridical rigour, but only its forms became significant for freedom. No wonder that Dicey thought England's law and freedoms were already gravely threatened. If its liberty hung on so slender a thread as the avoidance of new courts to deal with new kinds of cases, the end was indeed at hand. The one political issue that worried him very little was the consequences and the nature of war and the militarization of politics.[4] That was, of course, Montesquieu's overriding concern, and the events of our century have amply justified him. Nevertheless, it is Dicey's shadow that hangs over both the libertarian invocation of the Rule of Law and the radical attack upon it. One need think only of Friedrich von Hayek and Roberto Unger, for example, at present.

The other current adaptation of the Rule of Law also has roots in the last century. Its origins are in the court-centred American jurisprudence of Gray, but divorced from his positivism. The Rule of Law remains the rule of judges, but collectively and potentially individually, their decisions amount to a rule of rationality. It is not perhaps as coherent as Aristotle's rule of logic, but the resemblance is clear. Without some sort of political and philosophical setting such as Aristotle had provided, however, this new rule of courts floats in a vacuum. That is one of the frequently noted weaknesses of the late Lon Fuller's "inner morality" of law, and it afflicts those early essays of Ronald Dworkin in which Herculean judges maintain the Rule of Law single-handedly. Nor does the private law bias of these theories help to integrate into the Rule of

---

4 A.V. Dicey, *Introduction to the Study of the Law of the Constitution* (London, 1927), pp. xlii–xlviii and 324–401.

Law those aspects of social control that Aristotle's rule of reason had originally left to the masters of claimless people.

No defender of the Rule of Law has inherited more of Dicey's apprehensions than Hayek, but unhappily he has abandoned the latter's not inconsiderable historical learning.[5] In its place we get a theory of knowledge. The Rule of Law is necessary in Hayek's view, not because there are recurrent dangers of oppression and persecution, such as Montesquieu and even Dicey feared, but because of mankind's irreducible ignorance. Since it is impossible for us to predict the consequences or the form of the actions of each one of the members of society at any given time, it is also utterly impossible for us to plan our collective existence. Fortunately, if we set up general guide-lines that attempt no more than to keep us from colliding as we go about our own projects, we will prosper in spite of our limited knowledge. These governing guidelines are what Hayek calls the Rule of Law. Their main achievement is to facilitate the free market, but there are other benefits as well. By internalizing these minimal rules of social conduct we become more intelligent. Far from being anarchical a "spontaneous order" can be expected to emerge as individuals freely adjust their personal choices to these essentially "right of way" rules. Indeed, there is an evolutionary process that is set in motion by these numberless personal acts or adaptations. A natural selection of rules and traditions can be expected as the result of aggregate individual mini-experiments. This is, however, possible only as long as the rules are purposeless, that is, as long as they have no social end in view. They adjust, they do not order. They must only direct activities in order to avoid unnecessary conflict, collision and unwanted damage. Moreover, they must not be too rigid. For though predictability is the main end of such law, it must not stifle technological change, but rather, help people to adapt to its demands. Why that is not purposive political action is not clear. It is also difficult to see why we are able to plan the vast enterprises that have created modern technologies and the business and manufacturing organizations that realize them, if we are so ignorant of the probable future. Nevertheless, it is Hayek's belief that a "constructive rationalism" has since the early modern era misguided us into believing that we could plan our social future, and even regulate the market. It has inspired attempts to impose artificial legislation upon society which never realizes its stated ends, but does much to disturb and impoverish

---

5 See specifically, F.A. Hayek, *Law, Legislation and Liberty* vol. 1 (Chicago, 1973); Vol. 2 (Chicago, 1974), pp. 133–152; and vol. 3 (Chicago, 1979), pp. 104, 155–169. John Gray, *Hayek on Liberty* (Oxford, 1984), J.W. Harris, *Legal Philosophies* (London, 1980), pp. 128–139 and 245–251.

the "spontaneous order". This does not, however, seem to apply to the regulation of criminal conduct and law, about which Hayek is extremely vague. There we can no doubt predict, plan and even legislate. Of our ability to wage war we hear even less.

Originally Hayek thought that the continental legal code system was more suitable as a social facilitator, but eventually he came to see the common law as more likely to be slow but sure in developing those few but necessary rules to an ever-advancing economy. It was at one time capable of setting those formal and impersonal guide-lines which allowed the "spontaneous order" of the market to advance without impediment. Public planning for social purposes is not, however, the only threat to this Rule of Law. Intellectual arrogance is joined by primitive feelings of tribal loyalty and communal attachments that express themselves in nationalism to hamper the rational evolution of the "spontaneous order". The latter is not the work of mindless or affective individuals. On the contrary, it is the outcome of the choices made by the most rational members of society. For these do not exercise their intelligence upon public objects which no mind can encompass in any case, but limit their calculations to their own plans, which they can realize. They can do this presumably in spite of all those other agents of whose activities they must remain ignorant.

Hayek is quite right in refusing to think of himself as a conservative. He is no defender of authority or hierarchy, nor does he pine for those familial and communal traditions that the conservative critics of liberalism accuse it of having destroyed. His "spontaneous order" is in no sense related to these emotional bonds. His Rule of Law is not meant to unite society, or to give it common aspirations. Quite the contrary. It exists to prevent inefficiency, irrationality, irregularity, arbitrariness and ultimately oppression. For once the "constructive rationalists" who try to reform society discover that their artificial policies are doomed to failure, they invariably resort to totalitarianism in order to maintain their power and to continue their disastrous rule. This is not, in fact, how the fascist, Nazi or Soviet regimes of our century came about. Without war, ideology, the survival of military classes and values, and much more, these phenomena cannot even begin to be explained. But then Hayek offers no historical proof for any of his theories. They are the working out of his unfalsifiable assumptions about human ignorance and its necessary political consequences.

For legal theory the significant feature of this version of the Rule of Law is not just its abstractness, but its scope. General and impersonal rules are not there to protect rights, which Hayek regards as too rigid, nor does it serve the modest ends tied to an institutional order that Montesquieu had in mind. It does far more than to make the citizen feel secure from the agents of coercive government. It sustains the free market economy, and that "spontaneous order" is itself the foundation that all other aspects of the society as a whole rest upon. Everything else is derivative. This construct has not only no relation to any historical society, it basicaly implies that justice has been impossible under any other circumstances. At some remote time in the last century it is said to have prevailed, but as Dicey already claimed it was already in decline in Britain and in America.

The negative mirror image of the Dicey-Hayek model of the Rule of Law can be found among the radical legal critics of liberalism, most notably Roberto Unger.[6] For him also the Rule of Law is the entire legal order of the liberal state. It was in force until the coming of the welfare state, and its purpose and character were as Hayek describes them, but instead of functioning to protect a spontaneous order of any kind, it served to mask hierarchies and exploitation, and the destruction of the pre-capitalist communities. The overt inspiration of the liberal rule of law, according to Unger, is what Hayek takes to be its reality, generality of rules with uniformity of application, enforced by a judiciary separated from the rest of the government. And, like Hayek, moreover, Unger thinks that this system has failed and indeed never could have lasted. Indeed, it never was "real". It begins in early modern Europe as a bad bargain between the merchants and the monarchical bureaucrats who are already operating a stable legal code in order to stabilize royal rule. The merchants would have preferred to establish their own order of rules apart from this state apparatus, which would have been more responsive to their real needs, but they were unable to escape the embrace of the pre-existing bureaucracy. It was not a good deal for them, but it was the best bargain they could get. Their second failure was that they were never able to infuse society with the spirit of liberalism, so that their legal order could not achieve any degree of legitimacy. The pluralism of interest groups and the free market never could arouse the sorts of attachments that the religious and communal loyalties that liberalism had undermined could so easily summon. The Rule of Law was, therefore, from the first deprived of any basis of social support. Not that it deserved to be de-

---

6 Roberto M. Unger, *Law in Modern Society* (New York, 1976), pp. 52–57, 66–76, 166–181, 192–216 and 238–242. "The Critical Legal Studies Movement", (1983), 96 *Harvard Law Review* 563–675. See also Duncan Kennedy, "Form and Substance in Private Law Adjudication", (1976), 89 *Harvard Law Review* 1685–1778. David Kairys ed., *The Politics of Law* (New York, 1982).

fended, since from the first it was a mere mask. This reading of Max Weber passes for history, but, in fact, it is no less abstract than Hayek's account of the Rule of Law. It, moreover, agrees with Hayek's view of the incompatibility of primitive loyalties and the Rule of Law. Nor would there be any differences about the consequences of the judiciary being forced to choose between competing interest groups in the course of its procedures. Hayek would, of course, require them to stay out of such disputes, since it is not the function of his kind of legal order to get involved in making political choices. Unger thinks that this is inevitable, however, while Hayek merely thinks that it was a dreadful mistake that need not have happened. Interest groups could, in his view, have been left to work out their own problems. The result of the failure to leave them to it is what Unger calls "particularistic judgments". With that the fiction of judicial generality and neutrality are exposed for what they always were, shams, and any remaining public trust in the liberal Rule of Law must and should go. Nor can the governments of welfare states maintain the pretense that they are limited by rules. They do not merely serve one or another faction, they do so quite openly. In any case, the possibility that the Rule of Law might still be self-validating is destroyed by the realities exposed by both pluralism and the welfare system which reveal all the hierarchies and injustices of civil society. This is Hayek's lament and Unger differs from him only in regarding the collapse of the liberal order as a hopeful step to a far better political future. That the efficiency-minded and pragmatically open-minded policies of the welfare state spell the end of the Rule of Law was in fact already Dicey's message. The one question his heirs ought to answer is why citizens of Anglo-American and other welfare states are not as oppressed as he predicted they were bound to be.

In his later writings Unger has come to adopt an even more indignant tone in denouncing the Rule of Law. He now sees it, as he did not in his earlier analysis, as a pure ideological cloak that must be ripped off to expose the fraudulence of the entire ideology of the Rule of Law. As one of the spokesmen for "Critical Legal Studies", he now regards formalism, the belief in a gapless, impersonal legal system as the chief ideological screen behind which a "shameless" liberalism hides. In fact it is the servant of sinister interest groups, and its talk of rights is merely hypocrisy. That emerges as its most reprehensible public vice. The word ideology is moreover used here as a term of abuse that is meant to reveal the hypocritical and egotistical character of legal liberalism. A hierarchical and atomizing policy is the reality of liberalism, fairness and legal impartiality. The object of legal scholarship is to find the weak spots in the system and to put forward claims and to demand ever-new personal rights that will destabilize the whole system. The field of battle is to be the law school, where a co-operative union of teachers and students will set an example of how a more fraternal society would look. They would also suggest how less individualistic solutions to current legal cases might be devised.

That the reform of the law-school curriculum might alter American law is not a new idea. Case by case social renewal does imply a recognition that the legal system has a certain autonomy from the liberal political society in which it operates, an assumption that this critical and denunciatory analysis of the Rule of Law does not support. It is a protest that is in any case entirely within the tradition of American inter-generational conflict, which Samuel Huntington has recently described so well. It takes the form of a Manichean contest between the actuality of American politics and its promise.[7] And given the general cultural value attached to sincerity, especially among the young, the chief accusation is always hypocrisy. The call is for purity and there is a deep anti-institutional strain, recalling the creedal traditions of sectarian Protestantism. The hierarchies will eventually tumble and the American dream will be vindicated. It will also be a relatively painless transformation, since it will be conducted mainly through the existing legal structures. The success of this project is guaranteed by a simple faith in moral progress. From a functionalist social perspective one could argue that critical legal student-teacher ventures have served to sustain the existing legal profession by helping radical new college graduates to adjust to the alien and disliked culture of the law school and eventual professional world slowly and without too great a psychological cost. They have thus been eased into integration rather than hurled into it, which might have been far more disruptive for them and other people around them.

There is of course nothing new or odd in seeing courts and lawyers as members of the political society in which they perform both mediating and control functions as parts of a single political continuum on which other public agencies are also placed according to their degree of court-likeness or "tribunality".[8] It does not follow that courts do not have their own characteristic procedures or roles, nor that these constitute some sort of fraudulent charade to hide the actuality of oppression. The bench and bar have political tasks to perform and their practices constitute an

---

7 Samuel P. Huntington, *American Politics and the Promise of Disharmony* (Cambridge, MA., 1981).

8 Among political theorists see Judith N. Shklar, *Legalism* (Cambridge, MA., 1964), and more recently Martin M. Shapiro, *Courts* (Chicago, 1981) which again takes up the notion of a continuum.

integral part of an ongoing order. To judge one must obviously consider the viable alternatives and possibilities. This can be scorned as a craven "objectivism", devised to squelch the radical ardour of the pure. But why should one not estimate the current cost of innocence? That is not the utopian way of proceeding, and indeed Unger's vision, with its explicit rejection of historical argument, is not falsifiable or subject to deliberation. It is like all faiths, a take it or leave it proposition. In that it also resembles Hayek's view of the Rule of Law as a cure-all. For on the basis of his belief in universal ignorance it is just as impossible to know the consequences of *not* pursuing a given line of action as of pursuing it. The fact that X seems to have failed as a social policy does not mean that doing non-X is bound to be a beneficial course of action. That belief is also grounded on blind faith and oddly it also is a belief in human progress. It is, however, scarcely cynical in the latter years of our century to find such beliefs aberrant. This consideration ought not to be taken as a complacent assurance that the Rule of Law need not concern us, or that America is beyond reform. It does imply that destabilizing the existing system of civil liberties and rights, and the individualistic ethos that sustains them in the hope of building a truly fraternal order does not make sense. It shows little grasp of the fragilities of personal freedom which is the true and only province of the Rule of Law.

If Montesquieu's model has suffered at the hands of a historical theory, Aristotle has been abused no less. In his case also political and philosophical abstraction has done the damage. The rationality of judging, divorced from the ethical and political setting in which he described it, becomes as improbable as the liberal archetype when it is ripped out of its context. No two writers illustrate these difficulties better than America's two most representative legal theorists, the late Lon Fuller and Ronald Dworkin.

Both Fuller and Dworkin concentrate entirely on the rationality of judging, and especially as it is done by judges in the highest courts. The Rule of Law as the rule of reason is for both very much the expression of the authoritative judgments of appeals court judges, or often, of the justices of the United States Supreme Court. It has little to do with the realities of our municipal court system, especially as it operates in our cities. It is, however, not designed to describe the way the legal order actually works, but to demonstrate its rational potentiality, although this is not clear in Fuller's book, which often claims to be an account of the historical character of legal institutions. The point of significance for the notion of the Rule of Law here is, however, that rationality is to be found entirely in the arguments that judges must and do offer in defence of their decisions. While the emphasis on the rationality of arguments is

Aristotelian, the divorce of the judge from the normative and political context within which his ratiocinations take place is not. The result is a level of abstraction so high as to make these models politically irrelevant.

In Fuller's version the legal order seems to cover the entire governmental process in its scope. It does more than merely protect the free market as it does in Hayek's ideal world. Fuller's definition is far more encompassing. His Rule of Law is designed to cover all social conduct. And its "inner morality" is due entirely to its defining characteristics. Law must be general, promulgated, not retroactive, clear, consistent, not impossible to perform, enduring and officials must abide by its rules. Unlike Aristotle, Fuller did not specify what sort of society would be ruled by such a legal system, nor did he offer a very clear picture of its other historical institutions for social control and coercion. One may guess that he had not thought very deeply about any polity other than the United States. And as a legal ideal for us there is little to either accept or reject in this conventional list of lawyerly aspirations.[9] It is its moral status that, in the total absence of an ethical argument, seems unsure. Aristotle, after all, gave us reasons for the ethical and rational character and functions of the Rule of Law. In itself Fuller's inwardly moral law not only may, but has been, perfectly compatible with governments of the most repressive and irrational sort. The very formal rationality of a civil law system can legitimize a persecutive war-state among those officials who are charged with maintaining the private law and its clients. That was certainly the case in Nazi Germany, whose legal caste were perfectly ready to ignore the activities of the new court, police and extermination system as long as "the inner morality" of their law could remain unaffected.[10] The paradox of slavery, that made the slave both a human person, and the property of another, created a "dual state" in the pre-Civil War America as well, and it was just as irrational. No one can be three-fifths of a human being and two-fifths of a thing as the "federal ratio" had it in the original Constitution. Nor is the prohibition against murdering slaves, since they were people, compatible with their non-person status before the rest of the legal system, not to mention the exclusion

---

9 Lon L. Fuller, *The Morality of Law* (New Haven, 1964), pp. 33–94 and 152–170. "The Forms and Limits of Adjudication" (1978–79), 92 *Harvard Law Review* 353–409. Robert S. Summers, "Professor Fuller's Jurisprudence and America's Dominant Theory of Law", *ibid.*, pp. 433–449.

10 Ernst Fraenkel, *The Dual State* (New York, 1940), one of the few older studies of the Third Reich that remain valid. See also, Martin Broszat, *The Hitler State*, introduction by John W. Hiden (London, 1981), pp. 328–345.

from the guiding principles of the political order as a whole.[11] Such a legal system is as rational as the political order that it sustains. It may be a model of "inner morality" by virtue of the consistency and other marks of morality of the decisions of its judiciary, but it is still irrational. In a liberal society in the modern age slavery is irrational no matter how rigorously and impartially it is imposed upon the black population, and however free and secure its white citizens may be under a partial Rule of Law. The "inner morality" of the law far from imposing the rule of reason that it is supposed to create, may well serve to render political irrationality more efficient and more attractive to those who benefit from it. The "dual state" remains, moreover, a constant possibility in our century. Encouraged no doubt by its gradual disappearance in the United States, Fuller came to believe that law was bound in time to rationalize politics generally. Politics, he believed, is about purposes of the electorate and its officials and law structures these. There is here a theory of moral progress no less profound than Hayek's. It is, to be sure, difficult to imagine what else could sustain the notion of the Rule of Law as the proven agency of reason.

To an increasing degree the more recent essays of Ronald Dworkin absolve him from similar charges of political and historical fantasizing. It is clear that only a polity that has made a public and enduring commitment to something like the Declaration of Independence can be said to sustain his model of a legal rule of reason. He has not, in fact, singled that document out explicitly, but the primacy of equal rights, which is his basic norm, has no more enduring or better known public grounding. The Declaration may not be the law of the land, but it is surely not just any old pamphlet either. And when one considers the enormously reviving and invigorating role that it has played in the drama of political rights in America from the Revolution, through Jacksonian democracy, to Abolitionism and the implementation of constitutional rights since then, it is not fanciful to say that its function is to be an unalterable supra-legal source of justification for equal rights. It stands for a constant attention to the preservation and enhancement of equal rights by courts and citizens alike. It is not, therefore, the equal rights aspect of Dworkin's theory that is at issue here. It is his vision of the rule of reason generated solely by Herculean judges, in a political and ethical vacuum that is as troublesome as Fuller's "inner morality" of the law. Even with the justifiable assumption that in America, at least, though not in other political

---

11   Willie Rose Lee, *A Documentary History of Slavery in North America* (New York, 1976), pp. 175–223.

societies, rights are the dominant ethos, it is clear that the rule of reason cannot be sustained simply by the rational arguments that judges must offer in deciding both hard and easy cases.

The supremely competent judge in Dworkin's model of the rule of legal reason does not look, and his inventor does not look, at the political context within which he decides cases or that indeed generates the cases that come before him. He may live amid that mass of irrationality that is our tax and immigration law, the decadence of administrative agencies and the perpetual threat of and preparation for war, but the Rule of Law and the rule of reason will reign if judicial decisions are grounded in appropriate rules, principles and standards and rationally defended. The province of judicial action is indeed a very wide one. In choosing which of the two parties before him is right the truly knowing judge need not only look to rules to come to a rational decision, he may also ground his argument on the principles inherent in the political order of which he is a member and to its implicit standards of political morality. In doing so he does not legislate or exercise discretion, because his arguments are derived from a hierarchy of norms, not from considerations of policy, efficiency, or public welfare. Dworkin, of course, knows that policy choices can easily be translated into the language of principles. Indeed legislators and private persons do it all the time. The rationality of judicial discourse, nevertheless, does depend on this formally normative characteristic. As long as it remains within the limits of normative logic its rationality cannot be impugned.[12] Applied to a very limited group, and given the very specific ethical functions that Aristotle assigned to the Rule of Law, syllogistic judicial logic could well be said to have been the model for ruling by reason. But can it do so in the world into which Dworkin has pitched it, especially considering the kinds of controversies and political struggles in which his program must inevitably embroil the judiciary? The judiciary is not alone in claiming a rational standing, other agencies of government also have their share of "tribunality", that is, principled reasoned decision making. Even in terms of normative justification they may have rationally argued standards as grounds for not deferring to judicial decisions on rights or on anything else. Moreover while, indeed, every judicial decision grants and denies a claim, so do most political, and many private domestic ones. All these have a claim to rationality, but not to precedence. And few political struggles are more bitter than those that are fought over the question of "who decides?"

---

12 Ronald M. Dworkin, *Taking Rights Seriously* (Cambridge, MA., 1977), pp. 14–45, 81–130, and 291–368.

Once the members of the judiciary are involved in this sort of political struggle their claim to a special and higher rationality dissolves, however elegant and principled their decisions in specific cases may be. Indeed the erosion of public trust that such political struggles must bring with them is likely to prove far more debilitating to the judiciary than to other institutional agents, and so to diminish any rational strength they might bring to the political system as a whole. But that is only a policy-course decision. The rationality of the system as a whole is, however, crucial. The only political order in which the kind of principled reasoning that Dworkin attributes to the rational judge is possible at all, is of necessity a representative democracy, and as such it is particularly given to jurisdictional and open-minded interminable disputes. The ability of Hercules to prevail in such a polity depends less on the rationality of his specific style of argument than on his power, which is in any case what his name implies. The rationality of his office depends not merely on the rational quality of his decisions, but far more on his relatively aloof place in the political order as a whole. Moreover, others may well propose not only policies but principled arguments that are as rigorous as his own. The final decision between them cannot ultimately be settled by anything other than by political conflicts of uncertain outcome. Even if Dworkin were to identify reason and syllogistic argument as closely as Aristotle did, he could not without a comparable account of the process of persuasion in politics and of coercive social control show that the rationality of judicial decisions promotes the rule of reason throughout society, or even the legal rule of equal rights.

Is there much point in continuing to talk about the Rule of Law? Not if it is discussed only as the rules that govern courts or as a football in a game between friends and enemies of free-market liberalism. If it is recognized as an essential element of constitutional government generally and of representative democracy particularly, then it has an obvious part to play in political theory. It may be invoked in discussions of the rights of citizens and beyond that of the ends that are served by the security of rights. If one then begins with the fear of violence, the insecurity of arbitrary government and the discriminations of injustice one may work one's way up to finding a significant place for the Rule of Law, and for the boundaries it has historically set upon these the most enduring of our political troubles. It is as such both the oldest and the newest of the theoretical and practical concerns of political theory.

The Welfare State, The New Regulation, and The Rule of Law

Theodore J. Lowi

Between 1969 and 1974, the national government of the United States went on a regulation binge. Congress enacted and the President signed into law no less than 35 regulatory programs of fundamental importance to the economy and society. Even the seven years of the domestic New Deal with its 42 major regulatory programs surpassed this accomplishment by only seven and the super-active Kennedy-Johnson era produced only 53 such programs.[1]

One did not have to be a critic to look with astonishment upon the "quiet explosion in the scope and pervasiveness of federal regulation" experienced in the five years beginning in 1969.[2] But the second half of the 1970s, despite the unusual weakness in presidential leadership, appears to have been still more creative; as a consequence, it is possible to identify 130 major regulatory laws enacted in the epoch comprised by three presidents, Nixon, Ford and Carter. What makes this binge all the more significant is that this was a decade comprised of two right-of-center Republican administrations and one Democratic administration elected on an explicit anti-Washington, de-regulation campaign. Surely this means that the regulation of the 1970s was bipartisan, perhaps above parties altogether. For example, although there were some dissenting votes in House and Senate passage of the legislation, most of the votes were overwhelmingly favorable, and the dissents came from both parties. In other words, there was no clear partisanship; no polarization where all the Republicans were on one side voting negative and all Democrats

---

1 Gary Bryner, "Administrative Procedures: Political Origins and Policy Consequences" (Ph.D. Thesis, Cornell University, 1982).
2 William Lilley and James C. Miller, "The New Social Regulation", *The Public Interest* (Spring 1977), 49.

were on the other side voting positive. And this strong, bipartisan consensus cannot be explained on the grounds that legislators thought this was symbolic legislation which, to their surprise, was later made substantial by administrative implementation. Every single regulatory statute is deliberately large in scope and close to absolute in the results it imposes as obligations on the implementing agencies. Moreover, despite the wringing of hands all during the late 1970s and early 1980s about the unconscionable costs imposed by these new regulatory programs, few have been fundamentally impaired by deregulation. Even the most ideologically anti-regulatory President Reagan used his executive powers only to curb and to restrain regulatory agencies within existing laws; he made no serious effort to confront Congress with legislation repealing any of the new regulations of the 1970s.

WHAT'S NEW ABOUT THE NEW REGULATION?

The regulatory programs of the 1970s are called "new regulation" by those who sense something is different but cannot or will not put their finger on what is different about the typical regulatory program of the 1970s. Programs in this category are called "social regulation" by those who feel they know what that difference is. But those who agree that the appropriate designation is "social regulation" do not agree with each other as to what that means. Some, for example, consider this regulation new and social because it seeks to regulate private capitalist enterprise in a relatively antagonistic way in order to alter the relations among social classes of American society. Whereas the old-style "economic regulation" concerned itself with markets, prices, and specific aspects of wages and services, and usually within one specific economic sector at a time, the new-style social regulation should be considered class legislation because it cuts across the entire society, is antagonistic to capitalism, and is aimed at all of capital, all of labor, and the state itself.[3]

The applicability of this interpretation can readily be granted, but only for a few of the programs. For example, most environmental regulation programs will find labor and capital shoulder to shoulder against the legislation itself or against vigorous implementation of it. Class lines

---

3 Examples of this argument will be found in Charles Noble, "Rationalization of Social Regulation: Class Conflict and OSHA" (1982), in eds. Alan Stone and Edward Harpham, *The Political Economics of Public Policy* (Sage: Beverley Hills, 1982), Chapter 3; Paul Weaver, "Regulation, Social Policy and Class Conflict", in ed. Donald P. Jacobs, *Regulating Business*, (San Francisco, Institute for Contemporary Studies, 1978), Chapter 9.

are difficult to detect in CPSC laws and rules. Even on the one piece of legislation most likely to yield to a class interpretation, OSHA, Noble is rather tentative, as, for example, when he observes that "State intervention into the workplace has not galvanized workers around the politics of working conditions."[4] The best that can be said for this interpretation of the character of the regulation of the 1970s is that it had strong backing by the bureaucracy itself—that is, "the state"—and the bipartisan backing of Congress. It also had the enthusiastic support of a number of movements and groups not arising directly out of economic forces but out of experience with 1960s' breakdowns of authority, in areas such as civil rights, women's rights and Vietnam. Some of that energy was redirected toward environmental, quality-of-life, risk, and small-is-beautiful issues. This was definitely a "new politics", but the components of these movements and groups were overwhelmingly middle-class people who were definitely not arising out of or speaking for the working classes even when they were expressing their antagonism to capitalism.

A more sophisticated alternative interpretation is the argument that the 1970s' regulatory efforts were distinctive because they were designed to avoid or repeal the "law of capture" that had been articulated by the works of a number of political scientists in the 1950s and 60s, including my own. Their argument is that Congress sought to formulate clearer goals with specific timetables because the scholarly studies had demonstrated that broad and vague delegations of power tend to put agencies too much under the influence of the most specialized and best organized interest groups whose members were most in need of being regulated.[5] Unfortunately, this interpretation also fits only a small proportion of the regulatory statutes passed in this epoch. In fact, the only really clear case is the Clean Air legislation.[6] And even the Clean Air legislation is a doubtful case of clarity and specificity of law. Since it is an extremely long statute, one can find almost anything in it one is looking for; for

---

4 Charles Noble, "Regulating Politics: Conflict Over Working Conditions Before and After OSHA" (Paper presented to A.P.S.A. Meetings, Sept. 1–4, 1984), p. 18.

5 Alfred Marcus, "Environmental Protection Agency", in ed. James Q. Wilson, *The Politics of Regulation*, (New York; Basic Books, 1980), Chapter 8. Marcus mistakenly attributes to my work an extension of Bernstein's "life cycle" theory, when in fact I opposed that theory with the alternative one that agencies do not yield to capturing, regardless of their age, unless they are operating under broad and vague authorizations.

6 Bruce Ackerman and William Hassler, *Clean Coal/Dirty Air: Or How the Clean Air Act Became a Multibillion-Dollar Bail-Out for High-Sulfur Coal Producers and What Should Be Done About It* (New Haven: Yale University Press, 1981).

example, I treat it as an example of modern, open-ended and vague legislation because the 1970 Clean Air Act authorizes the EPA to establish air-quality standards in terms of the general requirements of public health, as the agency sees them. But even if we count the Clean Air Act as exceptionally clear in legislative direction, even the other environmental legislation, not to speak of the other "social regulation" of the 1970s, is broad and vague, specific only as to timetables.

Another theory has been developed around environmental policies but has implications for all the so-called new regulations of the 1970s. Schnaiberg, for example, distinguishes between two types of movements, a "politics of error" and a "politics of sin". For him, the former implies concern for resocializing individuals so that they can better appreciate the natural environment and its relation to human welfare—in broader terms, so that they can adjust their conduct in terms of their appreciation of the larger consequences of that conduct. The latter type of politics, according to Schnaiberg, attempts to "apply some coercive controls over the institutionalized forces that resist both environmental protection and social equity . . . . "[7]

This distinction has some real promise but requires redesign, mainly because Schnaiberg tries to cram all the coercive types of policies into the latter category when in fact there are very elaborate and important coercive policies in the former. The reason the distinction is so suggestive is that it really distinguishes between liberal policies and radical policies, where radical can be understood as policies of the ideological right and the ideological left. It also opens the analysis up to a developmental dimension.

Diagram 1 is a rendering of the results, where the "politics of error" and the "politics of sin" are translated into language that fits squarely into the legal tradition underlying liberal and radical (left and right) approaches to public policy. Traditionally, liberalism has been characterized by a very deliberate avoidance of morality in public life. Although each individual should have a moral code and live according to it, there are so many individuals, and each individual is so close to sacred that no one moral code can be put above another. Thus, as long as there is doubt— and to a liberal there always will be—as to the true and best moral code, no one code should be imposed by law upon others. Many liberals follow this moral position against morality so strictly that they are virtual

---

7 Alan Schnaiberg, "Redistributive Goals vs. Distributive Politics: Social Equity Limits in Environmental and Appropriate Technology Movements", *Sociological Inquiry*, forthcoming (p. 6 of the 1982 unpublished version).

Diagram 1—POLICIES AND PUBLIC PHILOSOPHIES

Public Philosophy	Policy Type			
	Regulatory	Distributive	Constituent	Redistributive
Liberal "Politics of Error" "Mainstream" Conduct Harmful in its consequences	"Cost-Sensitive" Reg. Old-style economical sector regulation Nation Standards Effluent taxes	Public works Pork Barrel Subsidies Research and data Sale of Exploration and Pollution Rights Services	Practical Education Categoric Grant to States National Standards for Local Implementation EIS to Improve Project "Causal Theory" for Regulation and Welfare	Graduated Income Tax Tax Credits for Growth or Environmental Protection Means-Tested Subsidies Unconditional Subsidies for Injury and Dependency Welfare Entitlements
Radical "Politics of Sin" Conduct good or evil in itself	"Cost-Oblivious" Reg. Shut-Downs Suits to Force More Reg. Citizen Surveillence of infractions	Publicly-owned Enterprises Appropriate Technology Subsidies Change-oriented Research	"Class Theory" Anti-Corporate Education Morality of Environ- ment Education Suits to stop public works EIS to convert Public Works to Reg.	Anti-Wealth Taxes Welfare Rights Punitive – Expropriation for Environment
"New Right" / "New Left"	Local Standards Protective Regulation Morals Laws Victimless Crimes Conservation for Civic Virtue (Parks, etc.) Corporate Self- Government	Public Charity Government Aid to Private Charity	Devolution to local government "Obligation Theory" Morality of Education in Public Order and Civic Virtue	Tax Write-Offs to investors Aid limited to "Deserving Poor" Sales Taxes

anarchists, opposing government controls in any and all circumstances. (In our day they are called strict libertarians.) But other, less orthodox liberals justify the use of government to the extent that it asserts its controls over conduct deemed *harmful in its consequences*. That does derive from a moral position that it is wrong for one person's conduct to harm another; but this is a different level of morality altogether, one which is settled strictly empirically in terms of the causal relationship between one set of actions and any outcome that can be plausibly argued as an injury or a cost. This gives liberalism an extremely strong affinity for science; and, except for the most extreme cases, it does permit liberals to live by their moral position against morality and at the same time embrace a fairly strong and positive government.

The contrasting position is one best associated in the United States with conservatism. That position is that it is possible to discover the best moral code, and once that is discovered, there is an obligation to impose it by law on others, not only to control their conduct but to make them virtuous. To put this directly in opposition to the liberal approach, conservative government is concerned with conduct deemed good or evil *in itself.* This not only characterizes the outlook of the Right but also of the Left, although the shared moral code of the Left is a completely different one, not merely an opposite one.

These "public philosophies" instruct their adherents in their definition of public problems and their choices of policies for dealing with those problems. This means that they will not only choose different policy approaches but will differ greatly on the problems that call for action—that is, the agenda. This makes the 1970s all the more interesting, because liberals and radicals came to similar conclusions about similar problems, proposed very different policies and found Congress, for reasons yet to be determined, receptive to them all.

Diagram 1 identifies a few examples of liberal and radical approaches to the problems of the 1970s. The diagram shows quite clearly that not all the approaches were regulatory. It also shows that not all the activity was generated by radical groups or radical movements using radical tactics. The diagram also suggests why it was possible for sophisticated and reasonable analysts to come up with such widely disparate theories about what happened and why. Radical approaches excite movements, and movement politics requires radical components of ideology to maintain high levels of emotion and low levels of organization. Radical approaches, no matter what the initial provocation, tend to see that provocation in the context of an immoral society, a conspiracy, or some other force generally aimed at depriving the world of justice. Inevitably, their policy proposals would either have a strong class component or be rationalized in a rhetoric dripping with class or system antagonisms. Liberal groups, even where they focus on exactly the same problems and embrace comparable policies, will be oriented much more narrowly upon the problem itself without too much concern whether a just society or system could possibly have tolerated the state of affairs giving rise to the need for the policy. Inevitably this would lead liberal groups toward identification of specific conducts, conciliatory relationships, and a willingness to take costs and other countervailing values into account. Thus, all the theories about the so-called social regulation of the 70s are correct, within specified conditions.

Although the diagram does help resolve certain inconsistencies of interpretation and tends to confirm the general framework that every basic area of public policy produces its own distinctive politics, there is a limit to its utility, as many critics have recognized. This limitation is that the policy/politics framework is not developmental. Introduction of the liberal/radical distinction adds an important dimension to the "arenas of power" analysis,[8] and that will be helpful in a developmental analysis. But in order to deal with how we got to the 1970s, we will have to step outside these cross-sectional comparisons and look directly at the history of government regulation in the United States and what values and perspectives were incorporated during the several epochs of regulation leading up to the 1970s.

ORIGINS OF NEW REGULATION: LIBERALISM, SCIENCE, AND WELFARE VALUES

Every society must develop a consensus on public philosophy to adjust continually to the following problem: How shall we allocate responsibility for injury? If the actual policies toward allocation of responsibility are difficult enough to describe in one's society, they are next to impossible to describe in societies of the past, including one's own.

The appropriate method is more akin to archaeology than anthropology. It requires careful evaluation of fossil remains and the piecing together of those remains into an approximation of the larger animal. Three types of fossils will be utilized here to answer questions about the prevailing values toward responsibility in the 19th century and how they de-

---

8 T. Lowi, "American Business, Public Policy: Case Studies and Political Theory", *World Politics*, XVI (4) (1964): 677-715; and T. Lowi, "Four Systems of Policy, Politics and Choice", *Public Administration Review*, XXXII (4) (1972): 298-310.

veloped into contemporary public philosophies. These are: 1. Legal concepts and practices; 2. Social science theory; and 3. Corporate concepts and practices.

The Law: From Individual Responsibility to Distributional Balance

The language of public policy in 19th century United States was laden with morality. The federal system reserved virtually all of the fundamental laws to the states, with local applications. The laws contained no distributional or cost-benefit analysis, little concern for ability-to-pay, and no expressed sensitivity to spillover effects. In those simpler days, communities met the fundamental problem of allocation of responsibility for injury with a relatively simple question: Who's to blame? The approach was not only highly moralized but also strictly individualized. In the terms laid out in the previous section, the 19th century attitude was conservative. In fact, federalism had made the states (and the local governments, which were creatures of the states) a house of conservatism; state law was responsible for the maintenance of property, contract, virtually all commercial intercourse, family and sexual practices, occupational regulation, education, community structure, water and land-use regulation, and so on.

The policy approach of "who's to blame?" also reflected prevailing institutional capacity. As Skowronek put it, 19th century America was a system of courts and parties, parties and courts.[9] The courts were the state common-law courts, whose jurisdiction extended to real cases and controversies, wherein no court could accept hypothetical cases or group/class cases. Individuals with material interests at stake must bring real complaints against other real individuals. There is no special significance to the fact that corporations were, and still are, legal persons.

Until well into the industrial revolution, some would say into the 1840s, formal cases of tort law were notably infrequent and unimportant. Cases involving questions of responsibility for injury were handled by more informal community and neighborhood mechanisms; and those that did reach the courts were likely to be handled under the principle of nuisance—which was hardly a principle at all but rather a concept embodying broad discretionary authority.[10] Nevertheless, the criteria in-

---

9 Stephen Skowronek, *Building A New American State: The Expansion of National Administrative Capacities, 1877–1920* (New York: Cambridge University Press, 1982).

10 Morton J. Horwitz, *The Transformation of American Law, 1780–1860,* (Cambridge: Harvard University Press, 1977), esp. Chapters II–III.

volved in those cases involved a strict code of personal moral responsibility which was carried over into tort law as that type of litigation spread: (1) Who can best bear the cost of development?; (2) The passive party has the stronger right; and (3) Conversely, responsibility should be borne by the party who set the action in motion. These criteria are highly individualistic, conservative, anti-development, in a word, anti-capitalist.

As commercial intercourse expanded, as more and more relations were handled by contract, as the laboring class expanded and mechanization spread, relations among strangers displaced relations among neighbors; formal relations displaced informal relations, and the number of tort cases increased accordingly. These were at first as severe as the pre-capitalist nuisance cases and informal community solutions. According to Horwitz, the courts "were prepared to award damages for injury to property regardless of the social utility or absence of carelessness [negligence]" on the part of the active party.[11] This individualized and conservative view of obligation went even so far as to interfere with the use of a contract of insurance to protect adventurers from losses resulting from their own negligence. In 1828, Chancellor Kent could state as "the better opinion" the principle that "the insurer is not liable for . . . . damage [which] may be prevented by due care, and . . . . is within the control of human prudence and sagacity."[12] This means that on into the 1830s, responsibility was so individualized that innovators and entrepreneurs could not, even by explicit voluntary contract and advance payment, spread and soften the injurious consequences of their own actions.

If there were to be development, new policies toward allocation of responsibility had to be fashioned, or no one would be willing to accept the burdens of risk. Thus, as the number of tort cases increased, the conservative individualism of tort law was changed in order to shift more of the cost of improvements to the injured parties. At least five legal doctrines helped adjust tort law to the requirements of economic development and mechanization wherein the innovator could either avoid or spread responsibility. A brief definition of each will be sufficient to show what the courts and laws were trying to accomplish:

1. *Incorporation*—inherent in the concept of the corporation is "limited liability."

---

11 *Ibid.*, p. 71.
12 Quoted in Morton J. Horwitz, *The Transformation of American Law, 1780–1860*, p. 202. See also Vivian Zelizer, *Morals and Markets—The Development of Life Insurance in the U.S.* (New York: Columbia University Press, 1979).

2. *Contributory Negligence*—even though the passive party may have the stronger right, a jury might be charged to acquit the defendant if the plaintiff (the injured party) acted in any way that could possibly explain the injury, such as being away from his normal post, having liquor on his breath, etc.
3. *The Fellow-Servant Rule*—juries might also be instructed to acquit wherever a third party, such as a co-worker, had anything to do with the line of developments that culminated in the injury.
4. *Voluntary Assumed Risk*—the injured party may find it all the more difficult to win damages if the dangers associated with the injury were made clear before the worker took the job or the skier got on the slope.
5. *Privity*—liability is generally limited to the immediate party to the contract for sale or service and does not extend to third parties, except where such gross negligence as the concealment of a defect can be shown.

The thrust of these doctrines was quite clearly to shift a much greater portion of the cost of industrialization to the victims—or at least to cast it off the risk taker.

Since these changes began to take place very quickly after the 1830s, they were in collision with the older and more conservative doctrines. In fact, the courts were caught betwixt and between. Widespread refusal to indemnify victims of economic change made courts in many regions extremely unpopular. Widespread displacement of workers by industrialization, the spread of injuries suffered by mechanization attributable to absentee owners, the displacement of farmers by commercialization of agriculture all contributed to social unrest and organized social movements that were able to identify the courts as agents of exploitation and expropriation. Courts naturally responded to this collision of values by engaging in "balancing". After all, judges were members of the communities which they served. They were aware not only of their unpopularity but the immediate cost implications of "widows and orphans". The "deserving poor" always had the right to local charity, but there were limits to resources available for charity. Judges were also aware of the fact that many of the injuries could be attributed to absentee owners and personal corporations who could afford to pay for a share of community burdens. Therefore, throughout the remainder of the 19th century, efforts were made to develop doctrines that balanced defense of the passive party against protection of the all-important innovator. The following are some examples of counter-balancing principles or strategies identified by legal historians:

1. "Last Clear Chance"—even where plaintiffs contributed substantially to their own injury they might still recover damages if they could show that the defendant could have avoided the accident. Although this doctrine "did not get very far in the courts before 1900 . . . it made a small, clear wound in the body of contributory negligence."[13]
2. *Res Ipsa Loquitur*, "the thing speaks for itself"—if the boiler of a train engine exploded without explanation, some courts accepted a *prima facie* case of negligence on the part of the operator (defendant) unless proof could be offered that negligence was not involved.
3. Liability without fault—a throwback to the early 19th century, this principle permitted the jury to hold owners at fault where they "set in motion some extraordinary or dangerous process" even where no negligence is shown.[14]
4. "Comparative negligence"—courts could soften the application of contributory negligence by a finding that it was relatively small in comparison to the "more gross negligence" of the defendant. Tried in the radical midwest as early as 1880, it re-emerged along with other softening doctrines in the 20th century.[15]

As common-law courts in various states began to engage in acts of balancing between contrary values in the outside world—as opposed to strict application of precedent—they began to look more and more like legislatures and this obviously invited legislative involvement. Some examples of legislatively imposed changes in judicial rules about who is to blame include the following:

1. Legislative abolition of the fellow-servant rule, in some states.
2. Legislative provision of workmen's compensation in some states, enabling governments to indemnify injuries regardless of negligence or comparative negligence.
3. Legislative imposition of safety standards, especially on railroads. No direct enforcement of these standards was provided, but if an injured plaintiff could show that standards were not being met, this made proof of negligence against the defendant easier to establish, even if the defendant could now show that his own particular injury was attributable to negligence.
4. Legislative experimentation with minimum standards of health and

---

13 Lawrence Friedman, *A History of American Law* (New York: Simon & Schuster, 1973), p. 418.
14 *Ibid.*, p. 14.
15 *Ibid.*, p. 418.

safety in the work place. Although the Supreme Court invalidated most of these early 20th century state legislative actions, they were nevertheless indicative of changing attitudes toward allocation of responsibility.

To bring the value changes up-to-date in the realm of law, it is only necessary to bracket in with two cases the difference between the pre-New Deal and the post-New Deal situation. The two cases in question are drawn from an area of tremendous importance in the consumer society of today, product liability. The first is a 1903 case appealed from the State of Minnesota to the Federal Circuit Court of Appeals. This is a *privity* case in which the local court held in favor of the defendant (manufacturer) on the grounds that since the injured plaintiff was an employee of the owner of the threshing machine and was not a party to the actual purchase, he was "a stranger to the transaction" and therefore had no remedy against the manufacturer. The federal appellate court reversed that decision and remanded it for further trial but at the same time actually affirmed the doctrine of privity even while identifying a small loophole through which at least a few plaintiffs, such as the one in question here, might nevertheless gain relief. The appellate court argued that "the negligence of the contractor or manufacturer will generally be limited to the party for whom the article is constructed, or to whom it is sold . . . . [T]here must be a fixed and definite limitation to the liability of manufacturers and vendors for negligence . . . " because causes beyond that which could be reasonably anticipated "insulate" the negligence of the manufacturer from the injury to the third person, except where there is a clear design defect known to the producer as dangerous to life or limb but is concealed from the users. The only other exception admitted by the court was one involving a "middle-man" such as pharmacist or dealer, where it was clear that articles bought by them would not be used by them or would make them suffer but would be passed along to the innocent consumer. But these exceptions affirmed in the overwhelming majority of cases the high degree of freedom of the manufacturer of responsibility for their product.[16]

Compare this to a 1944 case involving the injury of a waitress sustained by a bottle of Coca Cola which exploded in her hand by reason of some defect in the bottle or the pressure. Although the plaintiff could not show any specific acts of negligence on the part of the defendant, Coca Cola Bottling Company, the appellate court nevertheless accepted

---

16 *Re Balensi*, 120 F. 864 (8th Cir. 1903).

her claim that the manufacturer was liable. The chief judge affirmed for the plaintiff on the basis of the doctrine of *Res Ipsa Loquitur*. More interesting still is the argument of one of the judges in a separate concurrence:

> I concur in the judgment, but I believe the manufacturer's negligence should no longer be singled out . . . In my opinion it should now be recognized that a manufacturer incurs an absolute liability when an article that he has placed on the market, knowing that it is to be used without inspection, proves to have a defect that causes injury to human beings . . . *irrespective of privity of contract.*
> . . . Even if there is no negligence . . . public policy demands that responsibility be fixed wherever it will most effectively reduce the hazards to life and health inherent in defective products that reach the market. It is evident that the manufacturer can anticipate some hazards and guard against the recurrence of others, as the public cannot. . . . The cost of an injury and the loss of time or health may be an overwhelming misfortune to the person injured, and a needless one, for the risk of injury can be insured by the manufacturer and distributed among the public as a cost of doing business. It is to the public interest to discourage the marketing of products having defects that are a menace to the public [and] it is to the public interest to place the responsibility for whatever injury they may cause upon the manufacturer, who, even if he is not negligent in the manufacture of the product is responsible for its reaching the market. . . . The manufacturer is best situated to afford such protection.[17]

A 1978 products liability case brings the issue up-to-date. The plaintiff was injured while using a "high-lift loader" on a dangerous and uneven terrain despite the fact that the loader was designed explicitly for use on level surfaces. In fact the regular operator refused to work on that day because he was afraid of the uneven terrain; and his substitute, the plaintiff, "received only limited instruction" when he commenced work. The lower court held in favor of the defendant, but the California Supreme Court reversed and held in favor of the plaintiff on the basis of what the court itself called a "risk-benefit" standard. On the basis of this standard, the injured party "need not prove that the manufacturer acted unreasonably or negligently . . . " but only that the product falls "below ordinary consumer expectations as to safety. . . . " The case "must focus on the *product*, not on the *manufacturer's conduct*." Moreover, the judge and the jury should evaluate the effectiveness of the product in light of the product's "reasonably foreseeable use" rather than "intended use."[18]

Before going on to the other two categories of indications of the development of value systems in the United States, some preliminary

---

17 *Escola v. Coca-Cola Bottling Co. of Fresno*, 24 Cal. 2d 453, 150 P. 2d 436 (Cal. 1944).
18 *Barker v. Lull Engineering Co.*, 20 Cal. 3d 413, 573 P. 2d 443, 143 Cal. Rptr. 225, 96 A.L.R. 3d 1 (Cal., 1978). Emphasis in original.

reflections are called for. Conflicts in the legal doctrines of the late 19th century were fairly clearly resolved during the decades of the 20th century. We need more evidence to determine whether the conflict was resolved more in favor of the owner/entrepreneur or the injured worker/consumer. But a few other factors are already coming into focus. Clearly the move in legal doctrine was from private blame to public interest and also from individual responsibility to distributional balance. The direction was from concrete and specified conduct to the system of which conduct is a part. The direction of development can also be seen as one from intentions to probabilities, and from negligence to risk. In fact, as we shall soon see, the ultimate direction was away from negligence altogether beyond even the question of ability-to-pay to "social costs". But these observations are intended to be at a setting for interpreting other types of fossils.

Social Science: From individuality to interdependence

The remaining two sections on social values toward responsibility will be comparatively brief. The terms of discourse have been established. Moreover, there is an astonishing parallelism between values as they developed in the law and as they developed in social science theory and corporate practice.

Given what has transpired in the law, it would be shocking to find contemporaneous social science thought that was not highly individualistic. Americans did not have to know *Wealth of Nations* to resonate to Adam Smith's ideas. Although American social science of the 19th century was not the organized, professionalized and self-conscious discipline later to be seen in the form of AEA, APSA, etc., there were prominent social scientists in the late 19th century, and their views were distinctly individualist. Herbert Spencer's *Social Statics* is an example whose fame and representativeness earned it recognition in Justice Holmes's famous dissent in *Lochner v. New York*. Justice Holmes used the book as an example of social theories whose stress upon an individualistic view of contract, wages, labor, and the market could no longer prevail in the state legislatures attempting to enact laws regulating the safety and health of the workplace. As Holmes put it, "the Fourteenth Amendment does not enact Mr. Herbert Spencer's *Social Statics* [and was] not intended to embody a particular economic theory, whether of paternalism . . . or of laissez faire."[19] It was the laissez faire and its highly individualist perspec-

---

19 *Lochner v. New York*, 3 Ann. Cas. 1133, 198 U.S. 45, 25 S. Ct. 539, 49 L. Ed. 937 (U.S. N.Y. 1905).

tive that Holmes was attributing to Herbert Spencer. And Spencer was a highly representative case study. The social science historian Thomas Haskell sees the whole generation of mid- to late-19th century social scientists as one which viewed the individual as the "causally potent creature, normally master of his own fate and thus responsible for his own situation in life."[20] Dependence was viewed as the exceptional and pathological condition; the presumption of individual autonomy was very powerful. High position was evidence of merit, low position showed lack of merit.

This view carried over from the economic and social realm to the realm of health and well-being. Disease, like poverty, was caused either by providence or filth. The solution required improvement of individual conduct, which would clean the moral and physical atmosphere at the same time.

The change away from individualistic social thought received its strongest provocation from a public health phenomenon, the discovery by Louis Pasteur and Robert Koch of the germ theory of the causes of disease.[21] Germ theory probably had a moral effect on social thought comparable to the discovery of the New World and the confirmation of the theory that the world was round. There is tremendous significance to the realization that there is no individual moral responsibility for disease. People suffer through no fault of their own. We are all carriers, we are all murderers, and we are all victims. Proximate cause has little to do with the phenomenon. This is probably the first "systems idea" in modern social science history.

Totally aside from the causal importance of germ theory, the fact remains that the newly organized social science disciplines of the turn of the century shared a common assumption; in fact it could be considered the organizing assumption of modern social science: *the assumption of interdependence*. As Haskell put it, "The decisive experience of the first generation of professional social inquirers . . . was intense social interdependence and the habits of remote causal attribution encouraged by it."[22] Richard Ely, one of the Founding Fathers of the American Economic Association claimed that AEA was organized out of a rejection of laissez faire and an embrace of interdependence as the common denominator: "More and more we were becoming increasingly dependent upon others,

---

20 Thomas Haskell, *The Emergence of Professional Social Science* (Urbana: University of Illinois Press, 1977), p. 254.
21 Compare with Walter I. Trattner, *From Poor Law to Welfare State*, (New York: The Free Press, 1974), Chapter 7; the facts, however, are put to different use here.
22 Thomas Haskell, *The Emergence of Professional Social Science*, p. 252.

and more and more this dependence was becoming interdependence. The forces of life were getting beyond the control of individuals."[23] Albion Small, a founder of modern sociology, considered that "the justification of sociology was vortex causation." Perhaps that's the first use of jargon in modern social science, but it is extremely significant, inasmuch as it captures for Small and the others the idea that "social causation more nearly resembles a chemical reaction than a cable transmitting an electric current . . . [We] are convinced that every actual social situation . . . is a resultant of causal factors which run in on that center [vortex] from every point of the compass . . . "[24] Looking back from the perspective of 1927 on the founding period of social science, John Dewey put his own eloquent stamp on this basic assumption by his observation that "The new technology applied in production and commerce resulted in a social revolution . . . [It] is no exaggeration to speak [as Woodrow Wilson did] of 'a new age of human relations' . . . The invasion of the community by the new and relatively impersonal and mechanical modes of combined human behavior is the outstanding fact of modern life."[25]

These views drew from and contributed to legal and popular beliefs. But the important point here is not their influence but their very existence as evidence of the timing and character of the value shift. In both respects these views paralleled the legal developments. The timing of the change was late 19th and early 20th century. The character of the change was one from individual to collective, concrete to abstract, discreet linkages to system tendencies, and, eventually, from sensory experience to probability. "Who's to blame?" The question was becoming irrelevant—no longer an indication of the times but only a reflection upon the questioner.

Corporate Conscience: From Andrew Carnegie to Dale Carnegie

Andrew Carnegie is a good representation of the age of individualism in the market. Property and contract were absolutes—in the Constitution, more certainly in the minds of property owners and probably accepted by most non-property owners. It should be recalled that the eloquent language of Justice Holmes in the *Lochner* case was the dis-

---

23 *Ibid.*, p. 253.
24 *Ibid.*, quoted at p. 253.
25 *Ibid.*, p. 253.

sent. But Andrew Carnegie is also a good representation of the break-down, or rather the break-up, of property as we move into the modern capitalist period. Incorporation itself captures some of the modern real-ity, because it involves the softening of property through the subdivision and accumulation of units. But two other factors must be added to this to give meaning to the corporate experience in the present context. First, as the corporation was broken up into a larger and larger number of smaller and smaller units, it came to be publicly traded and therefore publicly (not governmentally) owned. In effect, the corporation was no longer owned "lock, stock and barrel". Ownership was more a matter of arithmetic than definition. Capitalism "split the property atom" in still another way by separating ownership from control, so that as own-ership was dispersed among many people, a large portion of whom were anonymous and some were only fictitious (corporations of various sorts who owned stock), control was concentrated in offices and boards of directors, where control could be based upon a very small proportion of the total stock in existence. [26]

Thus, just as courts had begun to speak of proportionate and com-parative negligence, introducing a continuum in responsibility, and just as social scientists were speaking of interdependence, so also was capitalism reducing property to a continuum, indeed to an interdepen-dent phenomenon. Corporate standing in law and politics and in ideol-ogy was bound to change. An equally profound transformation was tak-ing place inside business organizations; as Bendix observes, this change of ownership transformed the basis of authority. [27]

Ownership had become interpersonal and reciprocal. Accordingly, business ideology became more interpersonal. It had in fact become more political, more manipulative. As long as the boss was also the owner, the authority relationship was fairly clear and asymmetrical. Without the ownership base, the very idea of the boss begins to disappear. When ev-erything becomes a matter of degree, and authority itself becomes "inter-personal", the corporate animal looks a lot more like Dale Carnegie than Andrew.

---

26 Adolph Berle and Gardiner Means, *The Modern Corporation and Private Property* (Mac-millan, New York: MacMillan, 1932).
27 Rinehart Bendix, *Work and Authority in Industry* (New York: Harper Torchbooks, 1963).

THE LOGIC OF THE WELFARE STATE AND THE DEVELOPMENT OF REGULATION

The End of Personal Responsibility

All the fossils seem to point in the same direction, toward the same kind of animal. Diagram 2 attempts to give an approximation of it.

Diagram 2—ATTITUDE TOWARD ALLOCATION OF RESPONSIBILITY

A History in Three Dimensions

	1. Legal Ethics	2. Social Science Theory	3. Corporate Authority
A.	Discrete individual; blame & fault; personal liability	Discrete individual; free will, personal responsibility; status to contract	Discrete owner; property as dominion, "use-value"; "economic man"; ownership as basis of authority. Image: Andrew Carnegie
B.	Proportionate & comparative negligence; balancing	Dependent individual, impersonal forces; institutions & markets	Corporation as person; dispersion of ownership, separation of control from ownership; "limited liability"
C.	Cost and its allocation	Interdependence; multiple causation; social science as science	Property as continuum; political capitalism; organizational & interpersonal basis of authority
D.	Risk; negligence plus ability-to-pay	Causal models & correlates determining behaviour; beginning of systems thinking	Socialization of risk; indemnification of injury. Image: Dale Carnegie
E.	Risk/benefit; ability-to-pay plus ability to prevent; "public interest"	Systems thinking; new, accommodationist theory of consent ("interest-group liberalism")	Bureaucratization of authority; acceptance of welfare state
F.	No-fault	No-fault	No-fault

The general outline of the patterns seems to run from autonomy to interdependence, from absolutes to relativity, from concreteness to

abstraction, from discrete units to continua, from asymmetry to recip-
rocity, from liability to probability, from simple causation to systems or
"vortex causation". John R. Commons captures a comparable tendency
in his observation that the meaning of property passed from use-value
("physical things held exclusively for one's use") to exchange-value ("the
powers of acquisition reside in the ownership of things").[28] The corporation is the embodiment of this transformation; it is also the embodiment
of the transformation from property as ownership concentrated in a
single, personal owner to ownership dispersed among many highly partial, impersonal owners. What many sociologists and political scientists
have seen as the emergence of "corporate liberalism" can also be appreciated as "political capitalism", that is, the interpenetration of the corporation and the political system. All of this can be fitted into the several
logical steps that comprise the progression of American values regarding
the allocation of responsibility. The many striking parallels of substance
and of timing on Diagram 2 suggest that the changes presented in the
Diagram were interrelated and not independent of one another;
moreover, it suggests that they are reflections of a larger consensus moving toward a welfare state public philosophy before there was a welfare
state.

The following is a rendering of some of the logic that appears to
underlie the steps in Diagram 2. The judicial practice of balancing values
led judges directly toward a new ethical principle even if they thought
they were merely exercising political prudence. The step seems clearly
to be from absolute personal liability toward shared responsibility. This
was reinforced by social science ideas about dependence and interdependence, which were in the air at the same time, pulling the ethical principle
of shared responsibilities toward an escape from responsibility altogether:
that is to say, with joint or proportional responsibility, coupled with the
idea of interdependence, questions of blame rather easily became questions of cost. Once that has occurred, responsibility can be redefined as
a functional or economic relationship. Once again, insurance is a compelling example of the change of ethic in this century. The traditional ethic
was: "The law will not enable a party to recover compensation [through
a contract of insurance] for an injury, of which his own negligence . . . [has] been the principal cause."[29] Intimations of the new ethic
can be found at least by 1915: "In the age of commercialism, it is fitting

---

28 John Commons, *Legal Foundations of Capitalism* (New York: MacMillan, 1924), pp.
163–65.
29 Morton J. Horwitz, *The Transformation of American Law, 1780–1860*, p. 203.

and proper that everything, including human life be reduced to a money equivalent."[30] A more forcible statement is drawn from 1924: "The most important new development in economic thought will be the recognition of the economic value of human life . . . . "[31] These quotes are particularly interesting inasmuch as the prevailing view up to that time was that it was downright immoral to capitalize on something as mystical and religious as death. Since this secularization of immortality was a departure from the consensus view, the opposition to insurance continued to express concern for the immorality of measuring life or death by money and its contribution to the degradation of human beings. Nevertheless, the economic view of human life advanced, eventually to include the dependent whose capital value could be measured by the cost of maintenance, the cost of rehabilitation, and the cost of lost income.

Once these issues can be redefined away from questions of individual morality to questions of cost, it is a relatively easy logical step to move toward redefining responsibility itself, away from individual moral obligation toward probability (or risk). This is of course rendered into the actuarial principle in insurance, but, to quote Neil Armstrong, that can easily mask the "long step for mankind" represented by this "one small step for man."

All of this makes easier an appreciation of why the welfare state seemed so unrevolutionary by the time it was enacted into law beginning in 1935. All the logical steps to this point indicate a decline of personal responsibility, if not an end. Vice and corruption are no longer seen as the causes of poverty but rather its results. Poverty itself becomes the evil. Dependency no longer requires research into the question of whether the dependent person was deserving or undeserving; dependency requires only a calculation as to the relative cost of indemnification, rehabilitation, or maintenance. At such a point, personal responsibility can be replaced by public responsibility. This does not directly imply governmental responsibility but is consistent with it. And it is exactly what is implied by the *socialization of risk*.[32] Balancing between individual plaintiffs and defendants, deciding whether the innovator or the injured parties should bear the burden, was never a stable solution. By converting injury into cost and risk, and thereby socializing it, the

---

30 Vivian Zelizer, *Morals and Markets—The Development of Life Insurance in the U.S.*, quoted at p. 63.
31 *Ibid.*, quoted at p. 63.
32 T. Lowi, *The End of Liberalism* (New York: W.W. Norton, 1979), Chapter 10, although I failed to appreciate fully the significance of that concept.

opportunity arises where both parties can be spared. The proprietor/owner/innovator can be spared the cost of injury without displacing it directly upon the victim. Injuries can be permitted to happen by *indemnifying the victim*. The cost is spread to the whole society, and the injuries can be combined in a universe large enough to deal with its statistically (collectively, publicly). This also means that we no longer merely assume a system; *we actually create one*.

The bottom line of Diagram 2 anticipates an outcome not yet fully realized. But at least this much of relevance to the present inquiry can be asserted: the most widely shared social ethic, the modern position toward how to allocate responsibility for injury (and dependency), has relegated private responsibility to a minor role and has given overwhelming dominance to public responsibility. This means that individuals are permitted to escape personal responsibility or to provide for it by paying modest annual premiums. And more: since the ability to displace private responsibility is economically, and therefore unequally, distributed, government is drawn in to introduce equity in part or altogether. Thus, public responsibility comes easily to mean governmental responsibility, even though a large portion of the displacement away from private responsibility in the United States remains in the private sector. Whether private or public sector, risk has been socialized, responsibility has become public.

The Welfare State—A Brief Aside

It would be a mistake to stress insurance too much. I have used it here as a reflection of, or a fossil indication of, the decline of personal responsibility and the rise of no-fault ethics. It would also be a mistake to identify systems thinking in terms of its use in insurance. Although that is one kind of systems thinking, it is narrowly and technically a system in that each individual is defined as part of a statistical universe. Systems thinking, however, is used here in the much broader sense that it is a manner of thinking which seeks to define any particular item, event or problem in terms of some larger universe of which it is considered a part. All of this is part of welfare ethics without being synonymous with it.

The ethical basis of the welfare state was, therefore, fairly clearly established before 1935. The Depression only confirmed what had already become established in American perspectives about poverty and dependency as occurrences without implications of personal fault. The business cycle had become part of a germ theory of economic disease. Just as one did not have to know the specific germ to accept germ theory, so one did not have to have an elaborate analysis of the imperfections of capitalism to see it as the basis of economic ailments. And quite obviously, a person did not have to be a revolutionary to accept this theory.

This perspective explains why the welfare state did not appear to be such a revolutionary step. One could go so far as to say that we had killed free enterprise to save capitalism. But that was possible only because free enterprise was ethically dead already.

The original Social Security Act is a classic expression of the new ethic as it was embodied in 20th century liberalism. The 1935 statute contains eleven titles, seven of which deal with separate but strongly related programs. What is significant for our purposes is that each of these seven titles concerns itself with a category of injury or dependency that can be attributed to some identified weakness in the system of production or distribution. These include the aged and their survivors, the unemployed, dependent children, the blind, and the functionally unfit. Since each of these categories identified a regular source of injury and dependency, each title in the Social Security Act could be clear as to eligibility and obligation. Of equal importance for our purposes here is that each of these policies was based on an analysis of the problem and a theory about what kinds of economic conduct cause what kinds of injuries. This is at the very core of the liberal ideology as defined earlier; the welfare state is as pure and honest an expression of liberalism as can be identified.

Although a great deal more can be said about the welfare state, there is no place for it here and no need to deal any further with it. This brief discussion has helped establish three important points as context for understanding the development not of the welfare state but of the Regulatory State. First, the welfare state provides a vast amount of evidence that when the national government did begin to grow, it grew along liberal lines. Second, it helps establish that 20th century liberalism is compatible with the Rule of Law. Third, it shows that liberalism is not only compatible with science but is virtually unimaginable without science. A paragraph on each of these will be sufficient to lead us into the Regulatory State.

For the first century and a half under the Constitution of 1789, the national government was quite small, and its domestic policies were comprised primarily of cash subsidies and land grants, public works (internal improvements), and tariffs (which was also about all there was to our foreign policy). The purpose of these policies was to facilitate commerce, and the method common to these policies was patronage (or, in a more academic sense, distributive policy). Since there was in fact very little policy back of these activities, it is almost irrelevant to ask whether they were liberal or conservative. Patronage or distributive policies are quite clearly compatible with conservative *or* liberal administrations. Exceptions to this type of policy were few and far between until the 1930s when welfare state and other types of redistributive policies became frequent, as did regulatory policies. Since both of these newer types of policy (new to the nationl government, that is) were new in that they involved the national government in a direct coercive relationship to citizens, the question of liberal versus conservative ideology becomes pressingly relevant. And the answer is liberal. Virtually all the many policies that have been enacted by the U.S. Congress since 1933 are responses to somebody's analysis and theory about the causal relationship between some kind of conduct and some kind of injury or the avoidance thereof.

Many people, including apologists for the pitiful state of laws passed by Congress, argue that modern life is too complex and time is too short for Congress to pass laws that have any legal integrity at all—that is, where Congress states so clearly what its intentions are that administrators have good guidelines for their action and are not left free to make the laws completely at their own discretion. The 1935 Social Security Act deals with matters that were then and still are extremely complex, and the Congress in 1935 was working in a context in which they could not assume they had a lot of time on their hands. Yet, the Rule of Law in each of the titles identified above meets fairly well a Rule-of-Law requirement.

The third point, regarding the compatibility of liberalism and science, reinforces the second one. In this instance, Congress and the Executive Branch made very elaborate use of the best available economic and sociological analysis of the economy in order to guide it toward those regular occurrences about which a legislative rule can be drafted. Science was not used to tell Congress what to do, nor was science used as mere symbolism to overcome dissent. Science was used to meet the liberal obligation, which is to define harmful conduct and somehow to deal with it.

The Modern Regulatory State

Diagram 3—first constructed in 1967 and published in 1969, well before the great regulatory binge of the 1970s—reveals striking parallels between the phases of regulatory policy history and the phases of general ethical development as displayed on Diagram 2. Some of these were recognized earlier, but I had not then recognized the full significance of the general ethical context and how changes in that ethical context had fueled the changes in regulatory history.[33]

A certain amount of lag time should be allowed between the phases of Diagram 2 and Diagram 3. After all, there was some lag even in the states with all their governing experience as the policy process moved out of the common-law courts into the legislatures. There was to be even more lag at the national level first because there was so little experience at the national level with any regulatory policies at all, and second because there was widespread doubt that the Constitution would permit Congress to reach anything that was not very narrowly and formalistically defined as within the realm of "interstate commerce". Thus, at the dawn of national regulatory policy, 1887, the legal posture was heavy on morality, accepting without much translation the attitudes of farmers and small business people that monopolies were intrinsically bad. Specific trusts were identified, concrete conduct was identified concretely or was understood in the context of the antitrust cases in common law.

However, as we move through the 20th century, especially from 1914 onward (beginning with D. on the diagram), the perspective clearly changes toward the liberal in the treatment of conduct, and it also shifts toward the abstract, culminating in the embrace of the whole system of which any particular conduct is deemed to be a part. As this occurs, two additional things happen. First, the distance spreads further and further between the regulatory statute and the Rule of Law. This is indicated by the introduction of more and more discretion delegated to the administrators. It is also indicated by the increasing abstraction and open-endedness of the definitions of conduct to be regulated. What is not indicated on the diagram and was not fully appreciated at the time of its construction (and therefore not introduced among the characteristics) was the increasing involvement of science and technology in the regulatory-policy process. As the concept of regulation began to embrace "the system", science moved from analysis of particular causal connections between conduct and injury toward "systems analysis".

Systems analysis is an important, indispensable viewpoint for all the academic sciences, from the hard physical sciences to the softest social sciences. But that does not make it good for public policy; that in fact makes it dangerous for public policy. Apologists for the absence of legal integrity in modern legislation will argue that life has become too complex and time too short to permit legislatures to do anything more than to allude to a problem and turn the rest over to trained, professional

---

33 *Ibid.*, Chapter 5.

Diagram 3—THE DEVELOPMENT OF PUBLIC CONTROLS IN THE U.S.

An Analytic Summary

	SCOPE OF CONTROL	OBJECTS OF CONTROL	DEVELOPMENTAL CHARACTERISTICS
A.	The Railroads in Interstate Commerce (1887–)*	The railroads	concrete specific traditional rule-bound proscriptive
B.	The Trusts (1890–)	Oil trust, sugar trust, liquor trust, cottonseed oil trust, etc.	concrete general† traditional rule-bound proscriptive
C.	Goods (1906–)	Qualities of things. Substandard foods, impure drugs, immoral women, obscene literature, etc.	abstract specific traditional rule-bound proscriptive
D.	Commerce (1914–)	Relationships. Competition, fair and unfair. Qualities of commerce.	abstract general traditional discretionary prescriptive
E.	Factors (1933–)	Qualities of commodities behind commerce. Qualities of land, capital, labor and relations relevant to them.	abstract general novel discretionary prescriptive
F.	Exchange (1933–)	Qualities of relationships. Open-ended.	abstract universal novel discretionary prescriptive
G.	Markets (1934–)	Structures of relationships. Open-ended.	abstract universal novel discretionary categoric
H.	System (1946–)	The environment of conduct.	concrete universal traditional redistributive categoric

* Dates given may often disregard some antecedent, but these are provided only to suggest when a particular phase seems to have begun in earnest.

† The major innovation of each phase is underlined.

administrators who will spend a lifetime on that problem and that problem alone. But the fact of the matter is that life to a legislator in 1840 or 1870 was a great deal more complex *for them*, than our life is for our legislators. After all, they were having to cope with the height of the industrial revolution without any prior experience or tested economic theory. The concept of capitalism itself doesn't show up (according to the Oxford Dictionary) until the 1850s. And they were having to cope with modern cities before they knew anything about the causes of disease. Yet, there is far more legal integrity in the average state statute of the 19th century than the average congressional statute of the 1970s. One of the reasons for that is the conservatism embodied in so many of the state statutes. To impose a moral code on conduct requires only that one know the moral sentiments of the legislators and their communities. This takes very little research and no science. But even the liberal legislation of the 19th century also had greater legal integrity, and any liberal approach requires some research into causes and effects.

If this liberal legislation of the 19th century embodied more of the Rule-of-Law principle than today, there has to be a reason for that, and that reason seems to be that legislators relied more on sensory experience, legislating in reaction to specific conducts that were causing specific injuries or inconveniences. Their problems were complex, but their approaches were simple, from one simple hypothesis about conduct to one single statement as to its resolution. If our problems today seem more complex than theirs, it is *primarily because of the way we define our problems*. To insist upon seeing a problem in terms of the hypothetical system of which it is a part is to create complexity. Once the problem is seen from that perspective, it is indeed mind-boggling, so much so that it absolutely must be turned over to technical experts and professional administrators. But the complexity, let me repeat, derives more from the act of definition than from the intrinsically greater complexity of society in our time. The embrace by liberalism of science and technology helps explain why liberal legislation has grown more vast in scope with each passing decade. But at the same time, while science and technology have fueled this expansion, it should also be said that the expansion was happening anyway and drew science and technology into the process to meet political as well as intellectual needs.

Science and technology became increasingly important for liberal national legislation in order to develop the necessary analytic approaches, the methods, the concepts (GNP, etc.) and the vast data bases that were required for advocacy as well as implementation. Science was also drawn in to help develop the myths and symbolisms both to legitimize the vast programs and to overcome dissent with regard to them. That is to say, if there were to be no legal integrity to the policy, Congress needed to substitute for that some other kind of legitimacy. It is possible to be much more concrete about this argument that science in public policy quickly enters the realm of myth-making. First, there is no such thing as an actual system. It is an artifact of a general theory and a very large intellectual leap from experience toward that theory. What is the system around such conduct as walking on grass in a horticultural garden—*grassness*? What is the system around emphysema—*health*? If so, what is health? If the answer is "Health is the positive sum of a cost-benefit analysis," then we have simply gone from one myth to another. Cost appears to relate to a calculable factor; but even if we concede that cost is scientifically manageable even if science can never identify all the conceivable cost elements, what of the benefits side of the equation? Benefit involves definitions and decisions that go far beyond science toward the sorts of ethical choices that are uniquely in the domain of elected representatives of the people. Any science that accepts the job of identifying benefits has made itself into priesthood.

This is where we have gotten ourselves in the quest for our own answer to the question of how our society will allocate responsibility for injury and dependency. The transformation from private to public responsibility, from blame ethics to no-fault ethics, is very much alive in the liberalism that chooses to write the regulatory laws that it does and to defend them at one and the same time as good and as unavoidable. That being established, it is now possible to confront the binge of regulation of the 1970s and the special character of that legislation that makes it new.

THE NEW ETHIC, THE NEW REGULATION AND THE FUTURE OF LIBERALISM

The Epoch of the 1970s

Some would argue that the 1970s was an epoch of illiberalism[34] and there is an element of truth in that as long as it is still considered liberalism. The public philosophy of the 1970s was liberalism in its continuing concern for the consequences of conduct and its steadfast avoidance of commitment to a public morality. And it continues to be interest-group liberalism in that it continues to accept as legitimate any claim for

---

34 Harvey Mansfield, *The Spirit of Liberalism*, (Cambridge: Harvard University Press, 1978).

a public policy that can make a plausible argument about causes and effects. But it has gone beyond interest-group liberalism of previous decades because it has broken all barriers to expansion by its embrace of whole systems of conduct rather than specific conduct in relation to specific consequences. Regulatory policies adopted in the earlier epoch went after conduct on the assumption that its control would contribute to that extent to a better public order.

Regulatory policy of the epoch of the 1970s ordains the result rather than concerning itself very much with the conduct itself, and then it authorizes administrators to bring about the results by whatever rules or standards of conduct may by them be deemed relevant to the broadly defined outcomes. Thus, for example, the Wagner Act, probably the most ambitious piece of regulatory legislation in the older epoch, began with recognition of the need for industrial peace but proceeded to identify a fairly concrete list of conduct on the part of employers that would constitute unfair labor practices. The assumption was that control of those practices would contribute to labor peace. The same is true of the Taft-Hartley Act of 1947. It too was very ambitious and was characterized by labor interests as a gigantic piece of conservative legislation. Whatever the case, it simply added to the Wagner Act list of unfair employer practices of which unions and union organizers could be guilty. In contrast, note the language of another labor regulatory law, this one drawn from the 1970s, OSHA: "To assure so far as is possible every working man and woman in the nation safe and healthful working conditions and to preserve human resources." (Sec. 2B) A still more ambitious 1970s Act, the CPSC, ordained the newly established Commission to reduce unreasonable risk of injury from use of household products without ever identifying a single risk or suggesting how to make risks reasonable. In both these instances, after having ordained the outcome, Congress ordained that the respective agencies could set standards of behavior for employers and producers without providing any standards for what those standards would be. It simply assumed that the agencies would be able to discover the appropriate standards or would be able to draw them from standards already developed by the relevant trade associations. (In OSHA, these were called "consensus standards".)

Some have argued that the Clean Air Act is an exception in this period, in that it makes a special effort to define carefully and strictly the conduct to be regulated and the evils to be eliminated. Yet, even here, not all the expert students of environmental regulation can agree that the Clean Air Act is exceptional. For example, Alfred Marcus observes that "Air-quality goals were based on health-and-welfare criteria . . . " and that although "the federal government established air-quality *goals* . . . state governments set pollutant-discharge limitations."[35] In fact, environmental regulation was so broad that Daniel Patrick Moynihan, the Nixon White House liberal intellectual, felt the need to distinguish between program and policy, where "programs relate to a single part of the system; policy seeks to respond to the system in its entirety." When President Nixon set up the EPA and integrated environmental regulation, his message to Congress stressed the purpose of reorganization was to respond to the "system in its entirety." He went on to argue that "We need to know more about the *total environment*" if we are effectively to "ensure the protection, development, and enhancement of the total environment . . . "[36]

Thus, the most ambitious of the 1970s regulatory laws are in a direct logical line with predecessors but at the same time seem to escape the liberal orbit by ordaining the goals rather than the means. Regulation of relevance to labor had started out by identifying specific and concrete conditions deemed to be unsafe and advanced to other sets of conditions deemed to interfere specifically with the legislatively established right to bargain collectively. But the obligations and grievances set down in the law were relatively understandable in terms of actual experience. The same can be said of environmental and resource regulation. Earliest examples are found in liberal state legislation concerned with such problems as regulating the access to water of people living near rivers and streams. The larger "system" was expressed as "riparian rights", but the provisions were specific as to conduct. The same is true in such other environmental regulation as access to gas and oil in the ground. Since these fluids tend to move to the points of reduced pressure and the drilling of a well reduces the pressure, the incentive was on each owner to draw out as much oil or gas as quickly as possible to prevent it from flowing toward the well of one of his neighbors. The older common law of capture, under which the owner at the surface is entitled to draw up any minerals beneath his soil, was set aside by state regulations limiting production, rationing access, and maintaining maximum pressure so that a much larger proportion of the reserves could ultimately be drawn out. Interestingly enough, one of the last two congressional statutes ever invalidated as unconstitutionally delegating authority without standards from Congress to the executive branch was the "Hot Oil" Act of 1935 which gave the President authority to exclude from interstate commerce

---

35 Alfred Marcus, "Environmental Protection Agency," in Wilson, *The Politics of Regulation*, quoted at p. 277.
36 *Ibid.*, quoted at p. 277.

oil produced in excess of state regulations.

This should make unmistakably clear the distance as well as the direction we have travelled the past generation, and it should also confirm fairly strongly that these were logical progressions that were parallel across different sectors of regulation and parallel with the broader progression of social ethics regarding the allocation of responsibility for injury and dependency. But now the question is whether these outcomes were inevitable as well as logical. And I think here the answer is no. These 1970s regulatory statutes are irrational extremes produced by ignorance of the logic of liberalism and ignorance of the inherent weaknesses of liberalism.

Liberalism and Regulation in the 1970s

There should be no controversy over the proposition that every system of beliefs and of institutions possesses the seeds of its own collapse. Karl Marx was correct about capitalism but simply did not go far enough. All social systems are built on contradictions. The whole purpose of an institution is to balance certain contradictory needs, such as the institution of the family, which attempts to cope with the contradictory relationship between sex and the rearing of children—that is, between immediate and deferred gratification. Therefore, the question is not whether liberalism has such inherent contradictions but what they are and how to keep the contradictory elements in balance.

The inherent weaknesses of liberalism can be discovered by re-examining the original definition of liberalism especially in light of the ensuing development of perspectives toward social responsibility: liberalism embraces the individual and avoids the problem of different moral codes by concerning itself only with conduct deemed harmful in its consequences, avoiding as much as possible the question of whether conduct can be bad in itself. As reasonable, rational, and responsible as this appears to be, the basic weaknesses of liberalism arise out of those very virtues, because, *under some conditions*, all conduct can produce harmful consequences. This means that liberal government becomes responsible for all conduct. That does not mean that all conduct eventually comes under control, but it does mean that all conduct must under some circumstances come under surveillance. Through this process, liberal government becomes obliged to respond to any and every argument putting forward a case that a connection can be established between some particular conduct and some consequence seeming to flow from it. Sometimes the theory is backed by compelling evidence, such as the relationship between drunk driving and serious accidents. At other times, the theory is backed by only partial evidence or by statistical correlates rather than actual experience or laboratory tests. An obvious example is the relationship between smoking and cancer. At other times the evidence supporting a theory is a good deal more flimsy than that, as for example, where the effect may be twenty or more years following the hypothetical cause, or where connection may be clear but the threshhold or level of tolerance is not known. At other times the theory is weak because certain conduct or materials may be harmful when in the presence of one or more intermediate conditions. But the fact of the matter is that liberal government is now under pressure to make a substantive response—though not always enshrined in a new public policy.

Under these circumstances, liberal government becomes a gigantic magnet. Once the new social ethic has removed blame and socialized responsibility, everyone with any capacity has an incentive to compete over the allocation of costs, and there is no limit to what can be thrown in. Everything becomes good to do. Moreover, even though Thurow is correct in suggesting that everything about government is a zero-sum game, he tends to overlook the fact that a loss in one struggle (where a cost is imposed upon you) can be offset by a victory in some other struggle or by a reversal later on of all or part of any cost through the administrative process. Administrative procedures exist precisely to avoid locking in the costs of any earlier struggle. Jonathan Swift could have had the whole process in mind when he said, " 'Tis but a ball bandied to and fro, and every man carries a racquet about him to strike it from himself among the rest of the company."

The magnet's pull is strengthened by the indemnification built into the welfare state. The relaxation of priorities alluded to earlier helps explain also the very significant expansion of social security beginning in the early 1960s. There was, in other words, a "new welfare" almost a decade before there was new regulation. There are many parts to the story of the new welfare, and this is not the place to tell any of them, except to refer to the fact that they contributed to the gallop toward insolvency that was recognized by liberals as well as conservatives.[37] It is this explosive expansion of the welfare state that helps explain the epoch of new regulation in the 1970s. The explanation lies partly, but only partly, in the effort to reduce the cost of welfare. The other causal factor is more ideological, coming from the emergence of the new concept of "social costs".

Once government becomes a socializer of risk, and once it extends

37 See, for example, Lowi, *The End of Liberalism*, Chapter 8.

its responsibility to all conduct, *all injuries and dependencies, regardless of source or cause, become "social costs"*. I suspect that this is the origin of the concept of "social cost". Even where the theory of cause and effect is poorly documented, even where effect is difficult to define at all, the tendency would be to assert responsibility, not only because of the liberal's concern for consequences but also because of the new liberal's embrace of the total system of which each conduct and each consequence is a part.

The immediate meaning of this relationship is indemnification. This goes back to the original notion of welfare as articulated earlier, whereby we can escape the question of blame and hold the employer/innovator harmless as long as we are prepared to indemnify the victim. But that is only one side or one dimension of what can be done. This dimension is one in which we accept a given incidence of injury and indemnify all as best we can. The other dimension is that we can try to reduce the incidence of injury. And this we can only do by regulation, not by the general, categoric, redistributive techniques of welfare.

This reason for regulating is intimately involved in virtually all the 1970s "new" regulation. Not only can we hope to contain the cost of welfare by reducing the incidence of injury: no matter what the cost of regulation is *now*, the cost of the injury later, in terms of rehabilitation or maintenance or restitution, will be much greater. For one example, how often have we heard the educator argue that if we cut back on the pre-school program now, it will actually cost us more later in terms of remedial education, juvenile delinquency or crime. This is not to say that the educator is falsifying the situation. It may well cost more later. It is but an attempt to identify a particular mentality, in which there is a total and integrated budget for the whole system, regardless of the immediate costs, such as those of the manufacturer who is required to put a new scrubber in his smoke stack.

Add to this logic of the total social budget the mentality of the insurer; once the government became a socializer of risk it in fact took on the mentality of the insurer, even though no one pretends that all or any part of the welfare system is true insurance. But the mentality of the insurer definitely does exist in the present liberal government. Insurance is probably the only industry in existence in which the provider of the service is more concerned for the welfare of the consumers than are the consumers themselves. Automobile insurance companies are far more concerned about car and driving safety than are individual owners and drivers. The same can be said for the government as indemnifier or insurer. In fact, as with the automobile driver, the willingness to take risks is likely to go up as the consequences are insured or as the security seems to be improved. So, the insurers and indemnifiers may be chasing their tails but continue to try to regulate the incidence of injuries even as they maintain or improve upon the indemnifications.

Environmental Regulation—The Ultimate Case?

If a President Nixon could look to government as ensuring the "protection, development, and enhancement of the total environment," then quite possibly environmental regulation could be the ultimate case of liberal government. At the very least, it is surely a classic opportunity through which to view the future of liberal government.

First, let it be repeated that virtually all the regulatory legislation of the 1970s enjoyed bipartisan support, including the several important statutes coming within EPA jurisdiction. The few votes cast against any of the important regulatory programs of the 1970s were themselves bipartisan. Even the last of the highly ambitious environmental regulatory bills, which became the Toxic Substance Control Act of 1976, was adopted in the Senate 73 to 6 and in the House 360 to 35, with 22 Democrats and 13 Republicans on the nay side. This suggests—and the polls bear it out—that most of the new regulation was not only bipartisan but quite popular. The "deregulation" movement, which had gotten under way in 1976, was not an expression of rejection of government regulation but only of its inefficiencies and supposedly unnecessary costs. Surely this is why President Reagan sought his deregulation through pressure on administrators rather than by confronting Congress to get repeals of old programs or serious amendments.

A second observation worthy of repetition is that environmental regulation developed along lines parallel to the other areas of regulation and with the broader social perspectives toward responsibility for injury. This refers in particular to the ultimate embrace of the total system and the broad and vague articulation of legislative intent. But it included other parallels as well, with environmental laws always the more extreme in each category of comparison.

One of the most indicative and yet least appreciated features of environmental laws is the extent to which legislation attempted to compensate for the absence of legal integrity. This was done in combinations of three ways. And these are almost certainly harbingers of the 1990s and beyond in all areas of liberal government. These are: science and technical expertise; procedure; and overhead control. Each will be given a brief treatment.

The role of science and technology has already been well recognized here. But one of its most important functions needs to be stated quite explicitly. This is that scientific and technical expertise is involved in the political process mainly to overcome the constitutional problems of vaguely and badly constructed statutes. In fact, the presence of experts is the basic assumption of virtually all broad delegations of power from Congress to the executive branch. And we no longer even pretend that the expert will be relied upon to know what Congress wanted. We depend upon the scientist and technician to tell us what there is to want.

The first point takes on more substance in combination with the second—procedure. As a leading student of administrative law put it on the eve of the 1970s binge, although broad administrative discretion is unavoidable, that discretion "should be guided by administrative rules adopted through procedure like that prescribed by the federal Administrative Procedure Act."[38] That is the classic position, the classic rationalization of broad delegations of power and poor legislative drafting. In a brilliantly constructed dissertation, Gary Bryner has subjected procedures to a political analysis. By exhaustively analyzing such cases as the laws within EPA, he found that procedures, especially those that go beyond the Administrative Procedure Act, are designed: (1) to validate vague delegations of power; (2) to open access in order to co-opt citizens; and (3) to reduce the effectiveness of the programs themselves.[39] Each of these deserves a brief comment.

Procedure has been seen as an important saver of constitutionality at least since 1935, when the Supreme Court conceded that procedural provisions can validate broad delegations that might otherwise be struck down. But beyond that, it appears as though the broader the delegation the more elaborate the procedures. Bryner maps out the EPA rule-making process, showing that it is so laden with procedures that the typical rule requires 33 months from proposal to adoption. (His results are reproduced here as Diagram 4.)

The procedure-laden rule-making process has also had a significant impact on interest-group politics. Although the system still deserves to be characterized as "interest-group liberalism,"[40] the forms of activity have changed because of the expansion of procedural provisions. Where once lobbying of Congress was the predominant form of interest-group participation, nowadays participation of groups in the administrative process is equal to if not more frequent than congressional lobbying. I

---

38 Kenneth C. Davis, *Discretionary Justice* (Urbana: University of Illinois Press, 1971), p. 219.

39 Bryner, "Administrative Procedures: Political Origins and Policy Consequences".

40 Lowi, *The End of Liberalism*, Chapter 31 *passim*.

have been trying to coin a new word for it—*corridoring*. A further refinement on this change has been introduced by three constitutional historians trying to bring their analysis up-to-date. They argue that the 1970s regulatory legislation brought into government a new phenomenon, "issue groups". These are described as organizations concerned with public purposes rather than private profit. By the end of the 1970s there were more than 1500 such organizations, most of whose members were highly educated professionals "with considerable expertise and deep moral concern about a particular issue." Some economic interests were involved; many members received substantial consultant fees from government agencies "giving some truth to the old saw that reformers come to do good and end up doing well." But the common ties among members of these groups was a public interest tie. These groups have been officially included in the decision-making processes of the major agencies, especially of an agency like EPA. According to the authors, one of the reasons why the federal bureaucracy did not grow proportionally with the scale and ambition of these new regulatory programs is that the decision-making processes in the new regulatory agencies was "a kind of modern putting-out system based on federal contracts, that provided a technical information base to guide federal policymakers. And given the likelihood of an increase in the scientific study of social problems in the future, it appeared probable that the nexus between issue groups and government would continue to be constitutionally important."[41]

The authors recognize that this is a form of interest-group liberalism, but they are correct in suggesting that it is a special adaptation in which groups are more formally recognized as a part of the administrative policy-making process. It would be a mistake to leave the impression that this is the only occasion in which public-interest groups have been prominent. Groups of this sort were also prominent during the progressive period, and like the present ones they were composed primarily of middle class professionals who were more interested in reform than profit. On the other hand, they are correct in their observation that their formal involvement in administrative decision-making raises an important constitutional question about the legitimacy of public policy predicated upon the involvement of such private groups. There is a tradeoff here between private involvement in public policymaking on the one hand and the justification of broad delegations of power on the grounds that true experts of the public and private sphere can make the

41 Alfred Kelley, *The American Constitution—Its Origins and Development*, 6th ed., (New York: W.W. Norton, 1983), pp. 678–89.

best policies at the level of the administrative agency rather than Congress.

At this point should be added the third compensating element—overhead processes and control. There had always been a provision for overhead supervision through administrative and judicial review of agency decisions. That is the very essence of administrative law. But the new element, a significant innovation indeed, was the Environmental Impact Statement (EIS), and the requirement that one be filed well in advance of the onset of any project, showing its impact, its unavoidable, negative consequences, alternatives to the proposed activity, and any irreversible commitments of resources attendant to the project. This was to be an "action-forcing mechanism," ensuring participation opportunities to citizens concerned with their environment and the threat to it from governmental activities, especially public works.

Out of these new or newly enhanced provisions arise most of the distinctive politics of environmental regulation—and probably of most other governmental areas now and in the near future. First, these provisions have influenced the flow of mainstream liberal politics. The politics of regulation continues to be the most open and pluralistic but one also capable of bargaining toward an equilibrium highly favorable to the best organized. What the new regulation has done, especially environmental regulation, has been to open government up to a more radical, though still pluralistic, politics of the left. (See Diagram 1.) A carryover from the activist protest politics of the 1960s, we now have a large number of groups not activated by profit but are more like Madison's factions "actuated by a common impulse of passion." These groups are radical not because they are Marxist or adherents of some other revolutionary theory. They are radicals to the extent that they combine with their goals of environmental protection and personal security an attitude of hostility and distrust toward normal, mainstream politics and authority. To a large degree, this is a continuation of anti-Vietnam and pro-civil rights by other means. Other groups share with them a distrust of or downright hostility toward big organizations, including the big government in whose administrative processes they seek to participate. And they are radical to the extent that they see environmental issues as highly morally charged ones—for example, small is beautiful; capitalism is immoral; economic development has replaced infectious disease as the primary public health problem; etc. For most of these groups (as with 19th century conservative groups) a cost-benefit analysis is superfluous—and probably a sophisticated plot to perpetrate useless and dangerous public works on the people. And radical groups care little for "cost-effective" standards. They embrace "cost-oblivious" standards.

Diagram 4—THE EPA RULEMAKING PROCESS★

Phase I Start-up (One Month)

    Initial decision to begin a rulemaking proceeding
    Organization of working groups
    Preparation of background and preliminary materials
    Creation of public docket

Phase II Development (Six Months)

    Preparation and review of development plan
    Consultation with EPA management and technical advisory groups
    Consultation with external contractors and consultants
    Consultation with interest groups, other federal agencies, congressional committees
    Internal management review: Steering Committee
                                  Red Border
                                  Administrator
    Publication of Advanced Notice of Proposed Rulemaking in *Federal Register*

Phase III Preparation and Review of Proposed Rulemaking Package (10 Months)

    Working group preparation of proposed rule and supporting materials
    Internal management review: Steering Committee
                                    Red Border
                                  Administrator
    OMB review of paperwork requirements
    OMB review of proposed rulemaking package and regulatory analyses
    Publication of Notice of proposed Rulemaking in *Federal Register*
    Public comment period

Phase IV Preparation and Review of Final Rulemaking Package (20 Months)

    Working group preparation of final rule and supporting materials
    Internal management and OMB reviews—same as for Phase III
    Publication of Final Rule in *Federal Register*

Legislative and Judicial Review

★ This figure is based on an EPA study which found that before the OMB review process was instituted the total time to complete a typical rulemaking was 30 months. The OMB adds, at minimum, three months to the length of the process. Rules which are especially controversial will require considerably more time.

Mainstream and radical groups often make common cause in supporting new and more stringent regulatory rules by EPA, OSHA, CPSC, FDA, etc. All these groups are progovernment, shoulder-to-shoulder on these matters; if they differ it is most likely to be on the question of whether standards embodied in the rules are cost-effective or cost-oblivious. Although this distinction can be very divisive, it does not prevent the formation of coalitions of radical and mainstream groups against the large manufacturers. The emotional and highly redistributional rhetoric of radical groups should not obscure their fairly conventional tactics in matters of regulatory policy and rules.

A distinctive role for the more radical groups will be found in the collateral attack they make on industry, on local oligarchies and on mainstream political authority itself through the EIS mechanism and related strategies. It is here that some groups have created a "new politics" in appearance and probably in reality. Without question they are rattling if not weakening the foundations of older consensus politics, especially in the cities. Groups representing a new politics have made common cause with civil rights groups and some self-interested neighborhood groups to defeat major public works projects which, in former days, would have gone through without a squeak or a squawk.[42] The ill-fated Westway project in lower Manhattan is a fascinating case in point. This $4 million project combined rebuilding of part of the Westside highway with a vast redevelopment of the port area between 42nd Street and the Bowery. It failed, despite the fact that over 90 per cent was to be federally financed. Environmental groups combined with local reform (anti-party) groups and a few longshoremen's locals to beat City Hall. They had managed to convert a conventional "distributive" (public works, patronage) policy into a regulatory project by intruding environmental and land-use criteria. That is to say, the addition of environmental protection and land-use restrictions converted a public works project into a sanction for the enforcement of the environmental and land-use rules. This paralyzed, or I should pluralized, the city, delaying the project almost beyond redemption.

Similar forces have thwarted construction of new international airports,[43] new cross-town expressways and power plants. EIS and many other procedural requirements have opened up traditional policies to collateral attack, thereby undermining liberal consensus politics, reducing

---

42 Compare with Elliot Feldman and Jerome Milch, *Technocracy v. Democracy* (Boston: Auburn House, 1982).

43 *Ibid.*

the number and effectiveness of the few patronage resources left to the weakened political parties and contributing in various other ways to the inability of parties to absorb, placate or submerge these public-interest groups within political parties. Administrative procedures exaggerate this influence. But what is more fascinating to me about the new politics groups has been their ability to transform distributive policy into regulatory policy—to their advantage—through mechanisms designed primarily for enhanced participation and co-optation.

In the late 1970s, and not merely as a reaction against new politics, more and more mainstream environmentalists are joining with anti-regulation conservatives in support of "equity" approaches to regulation—with environmental regulation again leading the way. The primary technique is regulatory taxation, for example, the imposition of a system of "affluent charges" as environmental regulatory policy. This is an attempt, perhaps a counter-attempt, to convert moral issues back into economic ones. Thurow blithely asserts that "Environmentalism is not ethical values pitted against economic values. It is thoroughly economic."[44] Although that is a statement more of hope than of fact, it is nevertheless highly probable that such an equity approach to policy would undermine any public-interest movement, precisely because regulatory taxation, like any regulation, is so bargainable. It has the added virtue (or vice, depending on your point of view) of requiring no central cost-benefit analysis, permitting all affluent buyers the opportunity to make their own personal cost-benefit analysis. The fact that this and most other environmental, worker and consumer policies are regulatory prevents new politics groups from cashiering their redistributive rhetoric into redistributive policies. Their proposals generally boil down quickly into regulatory policies, which may be their short-run salvation and their long-run undoing. Westway exemplifies the short-run, to the degree that regulatory proposals can pull public works policies into the more dynamic regulatory arena away from the distributive arena. Their short-run success can also be seen in their effective participation in the administrative rulemaking process in those areas where the new politics groups actually support governmental policies. However, the very breadth of environmental and other modern regulatory laws permits the kind of coalition formation that has traditionally worked to the advantage of mainstream politics and self-interest groups. An unanswered question is whether the new politics groups have enough resources and emotional commitment to stay with this process as a permanent watchdog against

---

44 Lester Thurow, *The Zero-Sum Society*, (New York: Basic Books, 1980), p. 105.

capturing. That is part of the problem of the long-run.

Reflections on the Future of the Liberal State

In the 1970s liberalism collapsed. Jimmy Carter won the 1976 election with a campaign attacking the very national government over which he sought to preside. In 1980, a genuine, programmatic conservative was elected, for the first time this century. Among the many factors contributing to the collapse, an important one was the alienation of the American people from the national government. All of the public opinion studies document a steady decline of trust or confidence in the national government and its institutions beginning in the mid 1960s and extending into the 1980s. And without any doubt, one of the factors contributing most strongly to this decline of confidence was liberal excesses generated by the derangement of liberal principles.

Yet, it is equally true that while citizens rejected big government and its burdens, they did not reject the welfare state or welfare-oriented regulation, in the workplace, the marketplace, or in the environment. The same polls that document decline of trust and confidence also document the argument that voters only wanted to ease and shift the burden; even those who voted for the most radical of antigovernment propositions, Proposition 13 in California, confirmed in polls that they favored the important government programs but assumed the tax cut would simply force agencies to cut the fat and to provide the same services and security by being more efficient. This is no doubt the reason why President Reagan could slow and divert regulatory programs through administrative action but dared not confront Congress with requests for their repeal.

For the future of the liberal state, both positive and negative sides can be read in the events of the 1970s. On the positive side, the commitment to indemnification through the welfare state and to the reduction of the risk of injury and dependency in the regulatory state seem to be above partisanship and beyond repeal by momentary majorities in Congress. In other words, the major liberal accomplishments of the past generation seem to be institutionalized. Quite possibly one can add that public interest groups have contributed to the stature of liberalism by making it increasingly difficult to treat public works as mere patronage by requiring that each show explicitly how it serves some larger goals and avoids negative even if unintended, impacts.

On the negative side, the signs are also strong, probably stronger. For the first time there seems to be no interest group organized to support the Rule of Law. Academic lawyers consider it unrealistic. New politics groups are more concerned with getting a favorable administrative environment. Conservative groups oppose national regulation for mainly economic reasons and actually favor broader administrative discretion at local levels, where the administrators in question are police, prosecutors and often protectors of public order.

Once again environmental groups provide a good case study. Composed essentially of middle-class members, they are essentially from the same strata that always organized and fueled reform movements in the United States, whether liberal or radical. At an earlier time, these movements favored Rule-of-Law principles because they were seen as a good antidote to the arbitrary use of authority, whether that authority be aristocratic or bureaucratic. But at the moment there seems to be no strong sentiment among middle-class reformers or mainstream political activists to incorporate Rule-of-Law principles in their campaigns for new public policies. This is possible because the middle classes in the new groups are drawn from salaried strata rather than bourgeois strata; but for whatever reason, the middle-class members of these groups seem to have come to terms well enough with administrative discretion. They, like the corporate interests of earlier epochs, have begun to see certain advantages to themselves in dealing with a discretionary bureaucracy as opposed to a free-wheeling Congress. If that is the case, the prospects for a return to a Congress-centred government with a moderate and balanced bureaucracy seem dim indeed. It seems to be a truth more amazing than fiction that corporate interests or non-profit oriented public interests can accept science and procedure as a redemption for large and discretionary bureaucracies.

Without some effort to restore the Rule of Law to major redistributive and regulatory programs in the welfare state system, we confront not one but two and possibly three roads to serfdom. When Hayek spoke of serfdom in his classic essay, he had in mind a benign subjection to administrative authority along lines of the patron-client relationship or the vassal-serf relationship of feudal times. The cement of these relationships, then and now, is patronage—that is, the personalized use of resources. Administrative agencies working under broad grants of authority can be appreciated only as large structures of power with resources to use on a patronage basis. That is the secret of their success and their longevity. And that also helps explain why programs, once set up in professional, discretionary bureaucracies are so difficult to terminate or to guide. Liberal approaches, radical-left approaches and radical-right approaches all seem to be leading toward serfdom, precisely because the advocates do not appreciate the degree to which policies determine their own politics. Distributive policies, such as public works, are patronage policies that produce a dependency relationship between the agency and the clients, literally clients. Regulatory policies and redistributive policies tend to produce politics that are a great deal more conflictive and tend much more to encourage an autonomous, aggressive and healthily competitive relationship between government and the individual. However, regulatory and redistributive policies can be fairly quickly converted into distributive policies, with the attendant serf-like relationship, as the grant of discretionary authority to the administrative agency grows larger. This is because a grant of discretionary authority is patently an invitation to use the resources of the agency—whether money or privilege—to convert watchful and competitive citizens into dependent and supportive clients. I would argue that this is the entropic tendency in governments—the general tendency of governments to run down toward patronage policies and client relationships through the resort to delegations of discretion to administrative agencies.

Nevertheless, an epitaph for Congress and the Rule of Law would be premature despite the fact that its flirtation with death—that is, legiscide—sometimes seems to be life threatening. There is an urgent need on the part of mainstream activists and the more radical public-interest activists to re-examine the nature of policies and the politics likely to be associated with each policy choice. If Congress took this re-examination to heart, its laws would inevitably get better. If the apologists for legiscide are correct and Congress can no longer formulate meaningful rules and meaningful standards to guide administrators, then we can still study our retreat with care rather than simply capitulate into the merciful arms of the administrative state. All practicable roads to viable democracy— liberal, right and left—can lead to serfdom if due care is not given to the political consequences of each type of policy choice. This is not to argue for inaction. It is only to warn that any public philosophy, if unguided by a sense of its own limitations and some wisdom about the actual workings of government, will be its own undoing. That would be acceptable, downright enjoyable, if their follies didn't harm the rest of us.

The Intelligibility of The Rule of Law

Ernest J. Weinrib

I

The paradox of the Rule of Law is that it simultaneously states both an ideal and an apparent falsehood. As an ideal, the Rule of Law implies a contrast to the rule of men and evokes an image of stability, impersonality, and lack of arbitrariness. But as long as men have experienced the demands of law, they have also experienced in law the demands of other men. Law as we know it is neither spontaneous nor self-executing nor immune to change: its creation, administration, and interpretation are invariably acts of human agency and are exposed to all the mischief which human action can produce. If law inescapably implies the rule of some men over others, can a notion of the Rule of Law with its implicit contrast to the rule of men be in any sense intelligible or coherent?

The appeal of the Rule of Law is an appeal to the generality and impersonality of law. But it does not appeal to any and every form of impersonality. Historians have discerned in the earliest stage of Western law the achievement of impersonality through recourse to what were considered to be divine manifestations of judgment. Right, *jus*, was regarded as an element in a divinely ordained regularity,[1] and since the task of jurisprudence was to secure access to the appropriate divinity, the earliest lawyers were priests and shamans.[2] The resulting arrangements were, in their own way, an extreme expression of impersonality, which required that substance of legal determinations be immune to the inadequacies of human decision and which accordingly restricted the human role to technical matters of ritual and procedure.[3]

---

1 Benveniste, *Indo-European Language and Society* (1973), pp. 389ff.
2 This is especially well attested for early Roman law; see Schulz *History of Roman Legal Science* (1946), pp. 6ff. Cf. *Exodus* 21.6, 22.8 for Biblical law.
3 Birks, "English Beginnings and Roman Parallels" (1971), 6 Irish Jurist (N.S.), 147ff.

The Rule of Law which is relevant to modern and sophisticated legal systems is a repudiation of this version of impersonality. It takes for granted the momentous developments which transformed legal impersonality from an inescapable divine prerogative into a sphere for the operation of human intelligence. Sophisticated legal cultures recognize and celebrate this transformation. This is the point of the beautiful story in the Talmud, in which God miraculously intervenes in nature in order to settle a legal point and, when the divine signs are bluntly declared to be irrelevant by the jurists, reacts with the jubilant response, "My children have vanquished me, my children have vanquished me."[4]

What was absent from the sacral construal of legal impersonality was the possibility that there could be an intelligible connection between legal controversy and its resolution. The development of legal consciousness is the development of the awareness of the intelligibility of legal relations. Thus, legal controversy could be regarded as susceptible to better and worse resolutions: certain elements in the controversial situation could be viewed as having a more direct bearing than others, and the relevant factors could be discussed, analysed, brought into systematic relationship with one another, and generalized and extended to new situations. The impersonality of divine justice gave way to the impersonality of the exercise of human reason. Thus, Aristotle's seminal formulation of the Rule of Law is put in the following terms:

> He who bids law to rule seems to bid God and intelligence alone to rule, but he who bids that man rule puts forward a beast as well; for that is the sort of thing desire is, and spiritedness twists rulers even when they are the best of men. Accordingly law is intelligence without appetite.[5]

In this passage the Rule of Law is characterized in two ways: negatively in being differentiated from the rule of men, and positively as the embodiment of intelligence without appetite. The nexus between the two characterizations lies in complementary conceptions of man and law, the former as a conglomerate of intelligence and appetite and the latter as an expression of intelligence independent of appetite. Aristotle is here adopting for purposes of his discussion the Platonic version of the soul as a complex composed of intelligence and the two appetitive faculties of desire and spiritedness,[6] but whereas Plato argued that the primacy of intelligence could be realized only in philosophy, Aristotle regarded law

---

4 *Baba Mezia*, p. 59b.
5 Aristotle, *Politics* III, 1287a, pp. 29–34.
6 *Cf.* Barker, *The Politics of Aristotle* (1946), p. 146, n. 6.

as at least a possible sphere for the autonomous engagement of intelligence.

Aristotle's version of the Rule of Law is especially exalted and inspiring. His account implicitly disputes, for instance, the more recent view that the Rule of Law is essentially negative in that it merely avoids evils originating in the law itself.[7] In contemporary thought the Rule of Law is, to be sure, more than a bare assertion of the primacy of intelligence in law; it refers to a list of principles which bear on the legitimacy of certain modes of exercising authoritative power. These include the stability and prospectivity of legal rules, the independence and impartiality of courts and other tribunals, the procedural requirements of fairness, the publicity of legal proceedings and determinations, and so on. But if Aristotle is right, these elements can be looked upon as elaborations or specifications or realizations of the concept of the Rule of Law.

Now I want to dismiss for present purposes the issue of how these particular realizations work themselves out and to address the more fundamental task of showing the sense in which Aristotle might be right. Though almost all the elements of my position can be found in one Aristotelian text or another, I do not regard the task at hand as an exercise in exegesis or as the invocation of the authority of a thinker who dominated Western thought for a millenium and a half. First, as a thinker Aristotle has no more authority than is justified by the soundness of his thought. Second, Aristotle himself did not provide a comprehensive exposition of his legal philosophy, and his most striking insights about law received their appropriate elaboration only in the writing of Kant and Hegel. My purpose is not to provide a footnote to intellectual history but a construal of Aristotle's characterization of the Rule of Law that will reveal its significance for a contemporary philosophical debate.

The central issue in the modern debate is whether law is to be understood in instrumental or non-instrumental terms. Only in so far as law is conceived as non-instrumental can law be insulated from the purposes which might be projected on to it by political and economic interest. At stake is a conceptual point about the nature of law, not, in the first instance, an empirical one about the extent to which a given legal order realizes in practice the non-instrumental nature which its conceptualization as law may allow. The dismissal of the Rule of Law as necessarily ideological implies not only that law is an instrument available for exploitation by hierarchically entrenched groups, but that it can be nothing else. It denies the possibility that there can be *any* non-instrumental understanding of *any* set of legal relations.

---

7 Raz, *The Authority of Law* (1979), p. 224.

My argument will be that a coherent non-instrumental conception of law is especially to be located in private law. The set of relations governed by private law is singled out for two reasons. First these relations exhibit the most immediate and irreducible features of legal ordering. Whatever else law is, it is at least the sphere where claims are asserted by and against legally recognized persons. Even Marxists who are sensitive to the phenomenon of legal form have recognized private law as conceptually fundamental, in that public law can preserve its specifically legal nature only in so far as it reflects the form of private law even as it differentiates itself from its content.[8] It is *not* my point—as it was Hayek's,[9] for instance—that the Rule of Law is exclusively realized in private law and is in principle incompatible with distributive regimes. Nor is it my point that private law, because it is conceptually fundamental, is therefore to be preferred to public law. Rather, I wish to argue that in private law the non-instrumental aspect of law shines forth with particular brilliance, so that through reflection on private law we can grasp the Rule of Law as a coherent conceptual possibility. Second, in the law's self-understanding of its ordering of private relations, the role of "intelligence without appetite" is particularly conspicuous. Disputes between private parties are resolved by recourse to a disinterested and impartial third party who purports to work out the implications of their relationship by reference to a corpus of systematically interconnected principles and standards. This self-understanding has long been the subject of cynicism or incredulity, but it nevertheless forms the natural starting point for theorizing about law. Since private law presents itself as intelligible, it provides a ready point of entry for the consideration of the nature of the intelligibility of legal operations generally.

Let me return to Aristotle's text in order briefly to highlight its significance for the contemporary debate. As is well known, Aristotle is taking issue with Plato's view that rationality in political affairs can be achieved only if the governance of the community is in the hands of persons who combine absolute knowledge and absolute power. What must be appreciated for our purposes is that the difference between Plato's conception of the rule of men and Aristotle's conception of the Rule of Law contains a dispute over the relationship of law and thought. For Plato, law as such was a matter of convention, a particular set of norms, variable in place and impermanent in time which governed in

---

8 Beirne and Sharlet (eds.), *Pashukanis: Selected Writings* (1979) pp. 72–4; Kojève, *Esquisse d'une Phénoménologie du Droit* (1981).
9 Hayek, *The Constitution of Liberty* (1960), pp. 231 ff.

the empirical world the cave-like existences of particular societies. The paradigm case for the operation of law in these societies was an instance of injustice, the execution of Socrates. In Plato's view this event attested to a deep antagonism between law and philosophy, and much of his thought can be regarded as a profound philosophic commentary on the significance of this antagonism. The rationality of law could be achieved only if it were placed there by a legislator who had knowledge of transcendent truth. Law was rational only to the extent of the operation of intelligence upon it. For Plato the primacy of thought entailed the subservience of law.

Against this background one can appreciate the boldness of Aristotle's characterization of law as "intelligence without appetite". According to this formulation, law is not subordinate to intelligence; it *is* intelligence. Law is not merely pliable to an externally conceived ideal which is entitled to hold it in its mercilessly comprehensive grasp. Aristotle's conception of law is the fulcrum of his protest here against proposals for the rational restructuring of society which were the fruit of Plato's reflection on the injustice of Socrates' execution. It is similarly resistant to other political visions—whether beneficent or malign—which offer to overwhelm law as they remold society in reaction to specific injustice. Law is not subservient to external ideals because it constitutes, as it were, its own ideal, intelligible from within and capable of serving as a constraint upon the radical idealisms which postulate its depreciation. How can this be?

II

My claim is that there are legal relations which are immanently intelligible and can be grasped from themselves.[10] Now although all philosophy is the endeavour to disclose the intelligibility of its subject-matter, the notion of intelligibility has not itself been a preoccupation of recent legal philosophy. To indicate its meaning, I shall have to recall a mode of understanding which, after a long currency, has now fallen from fashion.

The intelligibility of any matter refers to a relationship between the

---

10 This claim is to be contrasted with that of Marx: "legal relations . . . are to be grasped neither from themselves nor from the so-called general development of the human mind, but rather have their roots in the material conditions of life, the sum total of which Hegel . . . combines under the name of civil society." (Preface to a "Critique of Political Economy", in McLellan (ed.), *Karl Marx: Selected Writings* (1977), p. 389).

matter's content and its form. When we seek a matter's intelligibility we want to know *what* the matter is. This search for the "whatness" of any matter presupposes that the matter is something, that it is a *this* and not a *that*, that it has, in other words, a determinate content. This content embodies the matter by limiting it: it sets it apart from other matters and prevents it from falling back into a chaos of randomness and unintelligible indeterminacy which its identification as a matter denies. The content has thus both a positive and a negative significance: it represents what the matter in question is and it differentiates it from what it is not.

The aggregate of elements which render a content determinate is, when considered in itself, the matter's form.[11] Form is the ensemble of characteristics which constitute the matter in question as a unity which is identical to that of other matters of the same kind and distinguishable from matters of a different kind. Form is not separate from content but is the ensemble of characteristics which marks the content as determinate, and therefore which marks the content as a content. Form and content are thus correlative and interpenetrating. If any content were formless, it would lack the very determination which would render it a something rather than nothing in particular, a content rather than an indeterminate existent. If a form, on the other hand, were without content, it would not be a form *of* anything and therefore not a form at all. The form of any matter discloses the intelligibility of its content, and form is to be regarded as the content itself under the aspect of its intelligibility. The elucidation of a matter's form is the disclosure of the intelligibility of the matter's content. Intelligibility resides at the congruence of form and content, and whatever is in the gap between them is either error or ignorance.[12]

---

11 In the twentieth century only neo-Kantian legal philosophy has paid attention to the epistemological significance of form. See, e.g., Del Vecchio, *The Formal Bases of Law*, tr. Lisle (1914), pp. 68ff, Stammler, *The Theory of Justice*, tr. Husik (1925), pp. 167ff. In "Fundamental Tendencies in Modern Jurisprudence" (1922–3), 21 Michigan L.R. 862 at 883 Stammler describes the "test" of form as follows: " . . . what elements of a conception are for other constituents of the same conception logically determining, in the sense that they cannot be left out of account if one is not to lose the entire mental representation which is directly under discussion, and vice versa? . . . "

12 " . . . What we have to do with here is philosophical *science*, and in such science content is essentially bound up with form . . . for form in its most concrete signification is reason as speculative knowing, and content is reason as the substantial essence of actuality, whether ethical or natural. The known identity of these two is the philosophic Idea . . . ." *Hegel's Philosophy of Right*, tr. Knox, pp. 2, 12. *Cf. Hegel's Philosophy of Mind (Encyclopedia of the Philosophical Sciences, Part III)* tr. Wallace, s. 383.

On this account, the intelligibility of legal relations requires the disclosure of the form or forms according to which these relations can be ordered and an evaluation of the adequacy with which particular legal arrangements express these orderings. The extent to which the content of a given legal decision is inadequate to its appropriate form is the extent to which the decision's intelligibility is defective. Such a decision can properly be subject to the lawyer's reproach that it "makes no sense". The intelligibility of the law's content, conceived as a matter of its adequacy to its appropriate form, I shall call, again following Aristotle, justice. In the next section I shall outline these forms of justice and indicate their bearing on the conceptual integrity of the Rule of Law. But first I wish to contrast the characterization of legal intelligibility as the interpenetration of the form and the content of the law with the approach which underlies much contemporary theorizing about law, and to signal some of the implications of this contrast for the issue of whether law can be understood in non-instrumental terms.

Form and content are, as we saw, correlatives: neither can be considered without the other and intelligibility lies in the recognition of their interpenetration. Much of the current theoretical analysis of law implicitly rejects this correlativity in favour of a one-sided approach whereby the theorist regards his task as the infusing into law of a justifiable content, without considering the adequacy of this content to an appropriate form of justice.[13] He will formulate some appealing proposal and demand of the law that it adapt itself to this suggestion. The literature is full of arguments structured on these lines: X is desirable and therefore the law ought to promote X. The identity of X might be wealth maximization or the promotion of utility or the restructuring of capitalism or the safeguarding of promises or the spreading of accident losses or the protection of liberty or the equitable redistribution of wealth or . . . Plato's *Republic* is perhaps the earliest example of this type of argument.

Also one-sided is the converse approach which postulates a form for law which is indifferent in its content. Attention to a contentless form

---

13 *Cf.* Hegel's observations: " . . . Form and content are a pair of terms frequently employed by the reflective understanding, especially with a habit of looking on the content as the essential and independent, the form on the contrary as unessential and dependent. Against this it is to be noted that both are in fact equally essential . . . . " (*Hegel's Logic* (*Encyclopaedia of the Philosophical Sciences, Part I*) tr. Wallace, s. 133). "We may of course hear from those who seem to be taking a profound view that the form is something external and indifferent to the subject-matter, that the latter is alone important." (*Hegel's Philosophy of Right*, tr. Knox, p. 2.)

is the characteristic of legal positivism, which restricts theoretical reflection about law as such to the elaboration of the nature of legal validity. In the positivist view validity is the mode of existence which is specific to legal norms,[14] and therefore theory can be concerned with law as such only to the extent that it is concerned with validity. Validity is an exclusively formal matter, and law is positive in a given jurisdiction only inasmuch as it has this form.[15] But when the formal quality of validity is regarded as the sole characteristic of what is legally existent, the law can have any content, and since the particular content of law is variable and contingent, it cannot rise to the level of significance for legal philosophy and it must be identified by the empirical traits of effectiveness and social recognition.

Each of these approaches is one-sided in its attention to either content or form, but they fit together in the following way. In the positivist model in which all that is intelligible about law as such is its formal quality of validity, law must have some content but no particular content. It is accordingly available to any content which the reforming theorist might suggest. The proposed content can become clothed with the form of law so that both are simultaneously present in a given jurisdiction, but since each is derived independently of the other, their combination is a juxtaposition only and not an interpenetration. The existence of a law, which is a matter of its participation in the form of validity, is regarded as something entirely different from its substantive merit or demerit. The proposed content is a content *for* the form but not *of* the form and they do not stand to each other as *each other's* form and content. The proposal is a detached reformism,[16] not in a psychological sense—reformers often evince a fanatical commitment to their own proposals—but in the conceptual sense that its particular content is not a substantive correlate of any formal requirement of law as such.

---

14 Kelsen, *Pure Theory of Law* (tr. Knight 1967), p. 10.
15 Kelsen, *General Theory of Law and the State*, tr. Wedberg (1946), p. 393. *Cf.* Hegel, "Prefatory Lectures on the Philosophy of Law" (1978), 8 Clio 49 at 62 (tr. Brudner): . . . Positive jurisprudence has for its content authoritative law, all the laws that have validity in a state, and that have validity by virtue of being posited. . . . We are here concerned, first of all, with the form of law as the latter is an object for positive jurisprudence: the content will be given afterwards. The form is this: the law is valid whether the content is rational and intrinsically just, or whether it is extremely irrational, unjust, completely arbitrary, and given by the authority of external force. The bare fact of being, of having authority, says nothing about worth. . . .
16 Fletcher, "Two Modes of Legal Thought" (1981), 90 Yale L.J. 970 at 984ff.

The positivist and reformist conception of the relationship between form and content in law bears in several ways on the notion of the Rule of Law. From the point of view of positivist legal theory, the Rule of Law cannot be an ideal because law as such is not an ideal but only a specific existent. The Rule of Law will obtain whenever the formal mechanism of validity has been effectively invoked, but this state of affairs is merely a matter of fact and is in itself neither desirable nor undesirable. In some versions of positivism there is gap between the effectiveness of a legal norm and the formal conditions of its validity,[17] and the Rule of Law might be understood as the coincidence of effectiveness and formal validity. This construal of the Rule of Law, however, does not ground an ideal but merely points to an equivocation in the theoretical structure of positivism. Nor can the Rule of Law be regarded as one of the virtues of law since in the positivist conception law has no virtue but simply is. The only property of law recognized here is the mode of existence known as validity, and the Rule of Law can, strictly speaking, be nothing more than the pleonastic affirmation that the existent exists.[18]

If the Rule of Law is to be an ideal or a virtue, its desirability must be ascribed to the reformist side of this conception. But from this standpoint the Rule of Law could be only a watery ideal at best. As an ideal it can represent only one value among many, and it therefore "has always to be balanced against the competing claims of other values."[19] Indeed since the legal side of the positivist-reformist conception is neutral to any particular content, the Rule of Law has no values of its own to throw into the scales and thus must always be dependent on values which are external to itself. On this conception the Rule of Law is intelligible only instrumentally; it has value only in so far as it forwards the values favoured by the reformer, and its status is hostage to his assessment of its usefulness.

This standpoint yields the following agenda for law and legal theory. Since law is merely an empty form which can serve as the receptacle for anything, there is no point to rummaging around within the law in search of a content. Such requirements as are to be found there—its "internal morality" to use Fuller's term—are nothing more than the considerations which make the social control exercised through law effective and which accordingly confirm the law's instrumental character.[20] What

---

17 Amselek, "Kelsen et les Contradictions du Positivisme Juridique" (1981), 35 Révue Internationale de Philosophie 460.
18 Kelsen, *supra*, note 14 at pp. 312ff.
19 Raz, *supra*, note 7, at p. 228.
20 Raz, *supra*, note 7, at pp. 223–6.

is central to reflection about law is not the recognition of a content adequate to the articulation of its structure from within, but the projection from the outside on to the empty form of law of a purpose which is independently desirable. Because this purpose takes its validity from the realm beyond law, it is not constrained by law but law by it; the law is at most a thesaurus of technical considerations which are subservient to the most effective realization of some particular purpose. The paradigmatic legal actor is the wise legislator who, like an architect, forms in his mind a plan for a structure which he conceives from the top down, with law analogous to the plumbing, necessary for the supply of water and the removal of waste but not something to glory in.

Theory has a two-fold task in this conception. First the dominant purpose (or set of purposes) must be devised and justified. The achievement of this purpose may require encouragement by government or the imposition of a sanction by a political authority, and a second theme is thereby suggested. Since the realization of the proposed reform requires political action, there arises the question of how the proposal stands with reference to the justification of the state and the legitimacy of state action towards a given end. Since law accomplishes the extrinsic purpose only through the state's monopoly on the machinery of coercion, legal theory is immediately conflated with political theory and law with politics. Accordingly all legal actors can be viewed as elevating, consciously or inadvertently, their political values to the status of enforceable legal norms.

This is not to say that all such extrinsic purposes are equally justifiable or meritorious. Rather my point is a structural one; it deals solely with the implications of different conceptions of the relationship between legal form and legal content for the notion of the Rule of Law. In the disjunction of legal form and content, law is restricted to the form of validity and is thus indifferent to a particular content which must then be infused into it *ab extra*. The intelligibility of this content is distinct from the intelligibility of law itself, and if law has any relationship to it, it must be that of means to end. But the Rule of Law claims that law can be its own end, and that certain content can be rejected as incompatible with law's inner nature. The concept of the Rule of Law can therefore not be sustained by the combination of positivist legal form and reformist legal content.

III

The positivist-reformist conception of law regards the content of law as a matter which is external to its form and thus allows positive law to be available as the instrument of any proposed reforming content.

In contrast, the conception of law in terms of the interpenetration of its form and its content renders the intelligibility of law internal to law itself. Legal form and legal content are not external each to the other, and neither is external to the law. Form is the aggregate of characteristics which determines the content as a content, as a *this* and not a *that*, and which differentiates content from the indeterminacy of featureless existence. Form is the intelligibility of content and content is the realization of form. Upon this reciprocal relationship no external standpoint is brought to bear. If this approach can be sustained for law, the intelligibility which it will yield will be one which is internal to juridical relations: law will be understood by reference to itself, and not by reference to something else. Now an instrumental understanding posits a relationship between the instrument and the end which lies beyond it. The extent to which legal relations can be understood in terms of themselves is thus also the extent to which the understanding of law as a means to some ulterior end is excluded.

No doubt the very idea of understanding something in terms of itself is problematic. The assertion of the possibility of such an understanding will be doubly eccentric in an academic environment dominated by the assumption that law is capable of being understood only in terms of economics or history or sociology or political or moral theory. An important feature of the internal understanding of law must here be noted. The understanding of law in terms of itself requires that law have a nature which renders it capable of such an understanding. The integration of the activity of understanding and the matter to be understood is impossible unless the matter is informed by thought, because only through the medium of thought can the relationship between the understanding and what is understood be reflexive. Law can be intelligible in its own terms only to the extent that it is in itself, however inchoately, an expression of intelligence, so that our understanding of it can be of a piece with its self-understanding.[21] In other words, only in so far as Aristotle's characterization of law as intelligence without appetite is correct will the non-instrumental understanding of law in terms of the identity of its content and its form be capable of achievement. And in this enterprise private

---

21 The status of the law's self-understanding is at the heart of the debate between Fuller and Nagel; see Fuller, "Human Purposes and Natural Law" (1958), 3 Natural Law Forum 68; Nagel, "On the Fusion of Fact and Value: A Reply to Professor Fuller" (1958), 3 Natural Law Forum 77; Fuller, "A Rejoinder to Professor Nagel" (1958), 3 Natural Law Forum 85; Nagel, "Fact, Value, and Human Purpose" (1959), 4 Natural Law Forum 26.

law is especially relevant, for in a sophisticated legal system such as the common law, private law makes a show of a self-contained rationality which marks it out as the natural starting point for the vindication of Aristotle's view.

To understand law as the interpenetration of form and content is to discern in law an internal dimension of intelligibility. The shape and extent of this indwelling intelligibility emerges from two convergent and mutually supporting movements of thought. On the one hand, one starts with the content of a sophisticated and developed legal system and distills its form from a consideration of its most significant features.[22] Since form is the ensemble of characteristics which make something intelligible as what it is, these features will be those which are so central that they must be understood if there is to be any understanding at all of the set of legal phenomena in question. In this first movement of thought they seem to emerge spontaneously as Archimedean points in legal consciousness, and even in the absence of a theoretical account of their ground or interrelation their centrality is certified by their invocation or presupposition in any intuitively plausible discussion of law. At the level of theory these are the features which must be explained or explained away, and any exposition which ignores them or does them violence runs the risk of being regarded as contrived or artificial or somehow amiss. And at the level of practice, legal discourse will incorporate or presuppose these features and will explicitly or implicitly recognize them as inescapably basic to the continuing elaboration of legal doctrine.

In our legal system, for instance, one can notice a variety of institutions whose pronouncements are authoritative sources of law. There are legislative, administrative, and adjudicative bodies which differ in composition, institutional structure, ranges of competence, and in the juridical status of the reasons which support their respective decisions. The resolution of a private dispute is accomplished by a retrospective judgment as to the propriety of particular behaviour, which judgment takes on wider secondary significance because of the requirement of systemic consistency, and this pronouncement is categorically different from a generalized direction addressed in the first instance to the community or to a segment of it by an explicitly political organ of government. In private law adjudication the court is presented with two parties only, a plaintiff and a defendant, and it is thus structurally cut off from consideration

---

22 Outstanding examples of this enterprise are Hart and Sacks, *The Legal Process: Basic Problems in the Making and Application of Law* (1958) and Dworkin, *Taking Rights Seriously* (1977).

of overall welfare. The inquiry is further restricted by the consideration that it is not everything with respect to these two parties which is relevant to the resolution of their dispute. The court regards the litigants' claims as assertions of right arising out of particular courses of dealings, and explicit consideration of the litigants' general attributes, moral character, social status, or material condition, is excluded.

These features, and others like them which I have not mentioned but which will be familiar to lawyers, rank as fixed points in our legal experience, and our reflections cluster around these points when we engage in the process of thinking law. This will no doubt seem suspect to anyone familiar with instances of legal scholarship in which the centrality of one or the other or all of these features has been denied.[23] Now this can be ascribed in part to a disjunction in such scholarship between the way we think *in* law and the way we think *about* law. In such scholarship, in other words, reflection about law is only externally related to the law itself. But part of the plausibility of this scholarship is due to the fact that the singling out of these features is at an intuitive level. Since these features are experienced as central even though no satisfactory or developed grounding of their centrality is offered, the assessment of their significance is vulnerable to the assertion of the holding of different intuitions.

The identification of elements in the content of a sophisticated legal system as fixed points of reference for the understanding of law accepts the content as initially given and then endeavours to draw out the form of law, the ensemble of characteristics which is the inward mark of its nature, by distilling it from the elements of content which are experienced as being fundamentally significant. In introducing these features, I mentioned that the progress from content to form is only the first of two converging and mutually reinforcing processes of thought. As long as the first process is considered in isolation, it is exposed to the charge that the inarticulate legal experience upon which it rests is the camouflage of an ideological or subjective selection for which there are no valid criteria. What confirms this movement from content to form is the extent of its convergence with the movement from the other direction from form to content, since intelligibility resides in the unity of the two elements of these converging movements. The possibility of this convergence is held open by the intimacy of the relationship between form and content. Since these two are internally bonded so that each is of the other, the difference between them is epistemological and not ontologi-

---

23 E.g., Posner, *Economic Analysis of Law* (2nd ed., 1977).

cal: form as the intelligibility of content and content as the realization of an intelligible form are not different entities but are aspects of the same entity which are held apart in thought in order to render the entity accessible to the understanding.

Since intelligibility lies in the interpenetration of these aspects, the products of the movement in the two possible directions from one aspect to the other will be congruent to the extent of the entity's intelligibility. The fullness of legal understanding is achieved only in the completion of both movements. The endeavour to discern the form in the content by selecting from the law the elements of content which are salient in legal experience will, in the absence of an elucidation and display of the form, seem to involve a merely arbitrary selection. Conversely the elucidation of the form of legal relations to which an adequate content must be found but which is not related to a concrete legal experience transforms law into what we know it is not, that is, a purely intellectual construct divorced from a social reality of interaction which is susceptible to legal governance.

The paradigmatic function of law is the ordering and direction of the external relations among persons. If the possibility of a non-instrumental understanding of law is to be sustained, the direction which law, provides cannot be regarded as an exclusively extrinsic imposition upon human interaction, because if it were only this, law would not be understandable except in terms of the purposes of those in whom this extrinsic imposition originated. Rather, the content of juridical relationships must be expressions of the forms of interaction which they govern. These forms of interaction are the conceptual patterns to which external dealings among persons can be reduced, and they exhibit the orderings which inhere in those dealings. As orderings, they capture the nature of the rationality immanent to interaction and they constitute the deep structures upon which the intelligibility of substantive legal rules depends. The law's direction of external relations among persons is intelligible in so far as it corresponds to and reflects the immanent rationality exhibited by these patterns. In its ordering of human interaction, law as an intelligible enterprise renders concrete and explicit an order which is already there. The intelligibility of law accordingly requires the disclosure of the possible patterns in the external relations to which law is to be applied. In Aristotle's terminology, these patterns are the forms of justice.[24]

One can distinguish two such forms, called by Aristotle, corrective justice and distributive justice, corresponding to the two modes of con-

---

24 Aristotle, *Nicomachean Ethics*, V 2–4.

ceiving of the external relations upon which law fastens. In corrective justice the relationship between the parties is that of the immediacy of a transaction, whether that transaction be a contract, a tort, or the bestowal of a benefit. In distributive justice the relationship between the parties is mediated by a scheme of distribution, and particular entitlements are a function not of a direct relationship between the beneficiaries of the distribution but of the criterion according to which the distribution is organized. Distributions embody what Nozick has more recently termed "patterning",[25] and justifications under distributions typically take the form "To (from) each according to . . .".

As Aristotle noticed, these two forms of justice are categorically different and this difference can be expressed in terms of the different notions of equality that each employs.[26] In corrective justice the parties, whatever their holdings or social status or character, are considered equal at the outset of the transaction, and this initial equality is preserved by transferring from one to the other the fixed quantity which marks the extent of the deviation from the transaction's implicit rationality. This sum represents either the plaintiff's loss or the defendant's gain, and in paradigmatic instances of restitution, gain and loss will be identical. As a conceptual matter, the single quantity which restores equality, must, to accomplish its function, be an appropriate intermediate point between two other quantities representing the transactionally relevant holdings of the plaintiff and the defendant. Its characteristic as a quantity is a reflection of the fact that in a transaction the interaction, being immediate, is

---

25 Nozick, *Anarchy, State and Utopia* (1974), pp. 155ff.

26 The distinction which Aristotle draws at *NE* V 1132a 1 is made perspicuous in Aquinas, *Commentary on the Nicomachean Ethics*, tr. Litzinger (1964), p. 950: " . . . He [Aristotle] says that the just thing that exists in transactions agrees somewhat with the just thing directing distributions in this—that the just thing is equal, and the unjust thing, unequal. But they differ in the fact that the equal in commutative justice is not observed according to that proportionality, viz., geometrical, which was observed in distributive justice, but according to arithmetical proportionality which is observed according to equality of quantity, and not according to equality of proportion as in geometry. By arithmetical proportion six is a mean between eight and four, because it is in excess of the one and exceeds the other by two. But there is not the same proportion on the one side and the other, for six is to four in a ratio of three to two while eight is to six in a ratio of four to three. On the contrary by geometrical proportionality the mean is exceeded and exceeds according to the same proportion but not according to the same quantity. In this way six is a mean between nine and four, since from both sides there is a ratio of three to two. But there is not the same quantity, for nine exceeds six by three and six exceeds four by two. . . . "*Cf.* Aristotle *NE* II 1106a, pp. 25ff.

between two parties and no more, since it is only in relation to two that there can be an arithmetically intermediate point.[27]

In contrast, a distribution embodies not the transference of a quantity but the fixing of a proportion. Distributive justice integrates three elements, the benefit or burden which is the subject of the distribution, the recipients among whom the benefit or burden is to be distributed, and the criterion according to which the distribution is to take place. The class of participants and the subject-matter of the distribution are notionally separate, and the entitlement of each member in the class to his share in the subject-matter is determined by the application of the distributive criteria so that, relative to this criterion, the entitlement of each is equal. Since the integration of the three elements takes the form of a proportion which can be continued without limit, there is no internal restriction on the number of participants: the more there are, the smaller the portion of each, and the fewer there are, the greater the portion of each. This is to be contrasted with corrective justice where the determination of the quantity which restores the initial equality requires two parties, no more (since there cannot be an arithmetically intermediate quantity between more than two) and no less (since if there were only one there would be no transaction and nothing to correct).

These two forms of justice are structurally different and mutually irreducible. They are as incapable of assimilation each to the other as are an intermediate quantity and a proportion. On this account justice does not in the first instance refer to a set of substantive normative principles, but rather points to the different structural features of differing modes of interaction. Corrective justice discloses the form of a transaction as the immediate interaction of two parties, and the proportional equality of distributive justice captures the structure of a distribution by indicating what distinguishes a distribution from a merely random confusion of persons and goods. The notions of equality employed by the forms of justice are, like them, formal and not substantive. Equality is a term of

---

27 In the tradition upon which I am drawing, the structure of pair-wise correction is represented in a number of ways: in Aristotle as the restoration of the antecedent equality of two lines (*NE* V1132a, pp. 25ff.), in Kant as effect and counter effect or action and reaction (*The Metaphysical Elements of Justice*, tr. Ladd (1965), pp. 35–37, On the Common Saying, "This May be True in Theory, but it does not Apply in Practice", in *Kant's Political Writings*, ed. Reiss (1970), p. 76), and in Hegel as negation of a negation (Hegel, *Philosophy of Right*, para. 97A). My formulation is closest to Aquinas' in his Treatise on Right at *Summa Theologiae*, 2a, 2ae, 61, 2 (tr. Gilby, 1975): "Here the equality will be according to an arithmetical mean, which lies between an equal plus and minus of quantities."

relation appropriate to justice as the ordering of external relationships, and its distinctive structure as a quantity or as a proportion is nothing other than the form of order which is to be discerned within a particular mode of human interaction.

Corrective and distributive justice, as forms of justice, represent the patterns which are internal to transactions and distributions. As archetypes of interpersonal ordering they exhibit the nature of rationality *in* their respective types of arrangement and do not refer to some external purpose towards which these arrangements ought to be oriented. Law is directive of these arrangements, and the task of legal theory is to elucidate a content which will most adequately realize these two forms.

A specific legal content is intelligible to the extent of its adequacy to the form of justice relevant to the category of interaction which the law is endeavouring to order. As a general matter (although I shall not defend this generalization here) adjudication of private disputes can be understood as the actualization of corrective justice, and the legislative and administrative direction of the community as the pursuit of distributive justice. This is not to say that the positive law of these domains is substantively just, but only that it is internally intelligible in terms of the conceptual structure of categories of interaction. The very point of the forms of justice, and what gives them their critical bite, is that they are forms; inasmuch as they set out the implicit patterns of interaction which illuminate law from within, they also provide a standpoint of criticism which is internal to legal relationships and is thus decisive because it cannot be deflected or escaped by a change of standpoint.

The integrity of the rule of law as a non-instrumental concept therefore depends upon whether either or both of these forms of justice is immune to the projection on to them of extrinsic purposes. Now in the case of distributive justice the imposition of external purpose is both possible and required. Distributive justice is the internal integration of persons and things according to a criterion of distribution, and the formal adequacy of the distribution will be a matter of the tightness of the fit between these three elements. But this internal aspect must be supplemented from the outside. Although the elements of distributive justice are internally structured, the identity and selection of the components of a *particular* distribution cannot be generated from within. Assume, for instance, that one wanted to replace or supplement tort law by introducing a distributive scheme of compensation. A decision must be made as to the class of injuries or handicaps or disadvantages for which compensation will be paid, the persons who will be burdened by the levies necessary to finance the scheme, the criteria by which recovery will be limited

if the need for compensation exceeds the available financing, and so on.[28]
Once such determinations are made, one can require that the various
elements fit with one another, but the notion of internal ordering is not
sufficiently powerful of itself to mark out the boundaries of the scheme
or the criterion of distribution.

In distributive justice the separation of law and politics cannot be
complete. The distribution must distribute something and it must distribute it to particular persons according to a criterion which can embody
an extrinsic purpose. The definition and particularization of the distribution cannot be insulated from the interplay of power, persuasion, sympathy, and interest which characterizes the political process. The role of
law is here restricted to vindicating the distinction between persons and
things which is presupposed in distributive justice and to attending to
the internal harmony of the elements of distribution by rectifying under-
inclusion and overinclusion. As the controversy concerning the judicial
review of legislation indicates, the boundary between law and politics is
not easily demarcated.

The argument that the Rule of Law is conceptually incoherent seizes
on the entanglement of law and extrinsic purpose in distributive justice
and generalizes it to all legal relations. But even if this entanglement were
inextricable—and I do not think it is—the move would be a mistaken
one in view of the categorical difference between distributive and corrective justice. Corrective justice makes explicit the pattern of immediate
bilateral interaction implicit in a transaction by treating each party as
initially equal and by affirming this equality in the transfer from one
party to the other of the quantity which represents the extent to which
the initial equality has been disturbed by the transaction. Since corrective
justice looks to a quantity and not to a proportion, there is no opportunity for orienting the relationship to an external goal through the selection of a distributive criterion and the determination of the subject-matter and the participants. Corrective justice adds nothing to the transaction
but the disclosure of its implicit character, and in a transaction each party
is accomplishing his own purpose and is not being directed to the
achievement of a collective but external goal.

Corrective justice is thus its own end, and it illuminates from within
the juridical relationships which exemplify it. It is a conceptual point
about corrective justice that it is intelligible solely in non-instrumental
terms, that to understand it by reference to something beyond itself is

---

28 *Cf.* Blum and Kalven, "Ceilings, Costs, and Compulsion in Auto Compensation
Legislation," [1973] Utah L.R. 341.

to transform it into what it is not and thus to fail to grasp it as it is. The ascription of an external purpose to a transaction is incompatible with the structure of corrective justice in at least two ways, each of which is a reflection of the consideration that by funnelling our understanding of the interaction through the medium of its ascribed purpose, we are denying the immediacy which is the defining feature of the parties' transactional relationship. First, since the parties to a transaction are each executing their own purposes, the best which the extrinsically imposed purpose can accomplish is to adopt a standpoint which is favourable to one of the interacting parties, but this preferential treatment of one of the parties would contradict the initial equality which is inherent in corrective justice as a distinctive form. For instance, the analysis of tort law in terms of possible aims such as compensation or deterrence[29] is incompatible with the understanding of tort law as the operation of corrective justice. The first of these aims is intelligible with reference to the plaintiff only and the second with reference to the defendant only, and yet the form of corrective justice postulates that each party has an equal standing and that neither is subordinate to the other or superfluous to their relationship.

The second way in which the projection of an external purpose on to a transaction is incompatible with corrective justice is that the purpose in question cannot be necessarily limited to the interaction of the two parties to the transaction. The purpose must embrace all those who fall under it, and from its point of view the immediate link between plaintiff and defendant is irrelevant. Since a transaction does not realize a collective goal, there is no necessary reason that the scope of the transaction should be coextensive with the operation of any purpose. Take tort law again as an example. If the purpose of tort law is considered to be the provision of financial support to those who suffer from personal injuries, the claim of this plaintiff can be no stronger than the claim of any person who is injured and who therefore falls within the ambit of the purpose. Similarly, if one conceives of the purpose of tort law as the deterrence of wrongful behaviour, there is no warrant for restricting the deterring sanction to those instances of wrongful behaviour which materialize in injury. The purpose as such is indifferent to the transactional context of the tortious injury.

In displaying the ordering which constitutes a transaction and which distinguishes it from a distribution, corrective justice reveals the inappropriateness of an instrumental interpretation of immediate interaction.

---

29 Williams, "The Aims of the Law of Tort", [1951] Current Legal Problems 137.

The transactional equality between plaintiff and defendant is unlike the proportion which characterizes distributive justice in that it cannot be oriented towards an extrinsically given objective. Private law can be largely regarded as the detailed and concrete elaboration by the authorita- tive judicial institutions of a content adequate to the form of corrective justice. To understand the content of private law in terms of the form of corrective justice is to penetrate the indwelling intelligibility of private law. As the realization of corrective justice, private juridical relations and the law which governs them can be grasped from themselves, and correc- tive justice sustains the possibility of a coherent and non-instrumental conception of the Rule of Law.

Corrective justice thus constitutes and exhibits the form of rational- ity indigenous to transactions and presents a structure of interaction which is immune to an understnding in terms of extrinsic purpose. It is important to grasp how deeply the non-instrumental conception of jurid- ical relations is embedded in this form of justice. The non-instrumental intelligibility of interaction presupposes a non-instrumental construal of action itself. The nature of the relationship between the parties points to and is grounded in a conception of the parties. This conception must now briefly be sketched.

Two features of corrective justice and private law come together here. First, it is a feature of both that they ignore such factors as wealth, virtue, or merit of the interacting parties. This characteristic, which was originally noticed by Aristotle,[30] has occasioned perplexity among philosophers. Hume,[31] for instance, explained this as an entailment of legal generalization, but this is unsatisfactory since generalization cannot, of itself, determine the features which are to be generalized. Second, the rectification worked by corrective justice is a restoration back to an initial notional equality. The quantity transferred from defendant to plaintiff represents the amount by which this initial equality has been disturbed. But this equality cannot refer to any particular property of the parties, whether it be need, merit, or status. In corrective justice the equality of the plaintiff and the defendant must be neutral to all the particularities of condition or character which mark their difference and their possible inequality.

The reason that the particular attributes of the litigants are ignored in corrective justice is that these attributes are not relevant to the transac- tion as such. In corrective justice their interaction is immediate, and there

---

30 Aristotle, *NE* V 1132a 2.
31 Hume, *A Treatise of Human Nature* (Selby–Bigge ed., 1978), p. 497.

is no place for the consideration of the varying degrees in which they partake of particular qualities and in accordance with which the mediating proportion of distributive justice might be constructed. In its ordering of external relations, corrective justice presents an extreme version of interpersonal externality in that it allows the internal characteristics of the interacting parties to be construed as irrelevant. All that matters is the interaction itself.

What allows the parties to be conceived as so completely external to each other is that they each are internally constituted as single persons who act and produce effects upon their circumambient worlds. The equality which corrective justice draws out of their immediate interactions is the equality that they owe each other as persons with an equal capacity for acting. In this conception, no single person is synonymous with his particular determinations: of no particular action can it be said that it could not have been otherwise. Corrective justice conceives of the parties as active and purposive entities. As such they are not determined to any given action or purpose, and the essence of their activity of their purposiveness lies precisely in their being self-determined. This capacity for self-determination is an abstraction from all particularity, and it is its very abstractness as a capacity which allows it to be equally applicable to all actors. In abstracting from the concrete richness of human particularity, corrective justice pays it the supreme compliment of seeing it as conceptually posterior to the operation of a self-determining will.

What has been outlined here as the ground of corrective justice will be familiar to readers of Kant and Rawls as moral personality.[32] Indeed corrective justice can fairly be described in Kantian terms as the point of view from which noumenal selves see each other,[33] that is, as the ordering

---

32 Kant, *The Metaphysical Elements of Justice*, p. 24; Rawls, Kantian Constructivism and Moral Theory (1980), 77 J. Phil. 515 at 525ff. It could also be termed (and its connection to my theme would be clearer if it were termed) juridical personality, not only because this conception of the person is presupposed in law but also because law is the most primitive actualization of the freedom which exists in its potential state in the person so conceived. *Cf.* Hegel, *Philosophy of Right*, para. 33–40 and Kant, *The Metaphysical Elements of Justice*, pp. 42, 69–70, where the bare possibility of the possession of objects in accordance with laws is called "juridical honour".

Of the two capacities which mark moral personality for Rawls, it is only the first, the capacity for a conception of the good, that is involved here. As for the second, the capacity for a sense of justice, private law, in the Kantian view which distinguishes justice from virtue, claims to be able to ground its coercion precisely on the conceptual irrelevance of any person's having or not having this sense. Even for Rawls, the two capacities of the moral person are not parallel: Rawls, *The Basic Liberties and Their Priority* (Tanner Lectures on Human Values, 1981), pp. 27–30.

33 *Cf.* Rawls, *A Theory of Justice* (1971), p. 255, characterizing the original position as "the point of view from which noumenal selves see the world."

of immediate interactions which Kantian moral persons would recognize as expressive of their natures. Law so conceived cannot be instrumental, because the Kantian moral person cannot be subordinated to any end which is inconsistent with his self-determining nature. Corrective justice makes explicit what is implicit in immediate impingements between persons, and in so doing it refers only to the person's formal capacity of purposive action while remaining indifferent to the background from which particular exercises of this capacity issued. Law conceived as the realization of corrective justice thus allows no entry to the instrumentalism of given purposes. In corrective justice law is intelligible as its own end.[34]

IV

In the richest understanding of the Rule of Law, law is intelligible from within and is thus conceptually sealed off from the interplay of extrinsic purposes emanating from the political realm. My argument so far is that the structures through which the law's immanent intelligibility can be grasped reveal the significance of Aristotle's view of the Rule of Law as intelligence without appetite. This argument has several strands. First of all, the presentation of intelligibility as the interpenetration of form and content stakes out for the understanding a vantage point which is internal to what is being understood. Second, law is regarded as the authoritative ordering of external relations between persons, and justice as the intelligibility of this ordering. Third, the intelligibility of law therefore involves the disclosure of the relationship between the law's content and the patterns of interaction which constitute the forms of justice according to which external relations can be ordered. Fourth, two different forms of justice can be discerned: corrective justice, which constitutes the internal rationality of transactions as immediate interpersonal impingements; and distributive justice, which mediates the relations among persons and between persons and things according to some criterion. Fifth, these two forms evince differing structures and they are not reducible one to the other. Sixth, the structure of distributive justice reveals the amenability of distributive arrangements to extrinsic purposes, whereas the structure of corrective justice is immune to such purposes. Seventh, corrective justice presupposes the formal equality of Kantian moral persons which abstracts from the particularity of specific purposes and circumstances to the capacity for rights which inheres in purposiveness it-

---

34 *Cf.* Aristotle, *NE* I 1094a 4 on activities which are their own ends.

self. Eighth, the law whose content is adequate to the form of corrective justice is, as such, intelligible from within and only from within. In the transactional relationships of corrective justice which are largely governed by private law, the non-instrumental intelligibiity of the Rule of Law can be fully realized.

The significance of Aristotle's characterization of law as intelligence without appetite can now be appreciated. Law makes explicit the patterns which constitute the implicit rationality of interaction by specifying the content for the appropriate form of justice. The form provides the deep structure which is realized in the legal content and through which the content can be understood. The working out of the content in accordance with the implicit contours of its own intelligibility is itself an exhibition of intelligence. Since the intelligibility of any matter is located in the interpenetration of its form and its content, the grasp of legal relations in terms of their own intelligibility is the understanding of thought in the only way it can truly be understood, through thinking. In corrective justice especially, where the projection of extrinsic purpose finds no place, the relationship between the understanding and what is understood is a particularly intimate one. The task of the adjudicator in a private law dispute is to follow through and give specificity to the order implicit in the nature of transactions, and his reasons for judgment are the public announcement of how he construes the intimations of this order in the context of a particular occurrence. This understanding of private law is reflected in the common law's self-understanding of the adjudicative process which regards the judge's decision not as the exercise of a political choice but as an act of cognition.

This non-instrumental view of private law in terms of the indwelling intelligibility of corrective justice is avowedly and unabashedly conceptual. Now one might be tempted to object that this conceptualism is barren and abstract, and that in so far as it hermetically seals law off from the reality which informs it, it distorts the nature of what it purports to understand. Of course, in every dispute having ideological overtones, there is a temptation pre-emptively to occupy the high ground of reality and so gain a favoured vantage point for the criticism of opposing views.[35] But the forms of justice being invoked here are not forms in the Platonic sense which lie, as Plato said of the form of the good, "on the

---

35 *Cf.* Shell, *The Economy of Literature* (1978), p. 1: . . . Those discourses are ideological that argue or assume that matter is ontologically prior to thought. . . . Every ideology would demonstrate that all other ideologies are idealist expressions of the basic matter to which it alone has real access. . . .

other side of being".[36] Rather their acccount of the law as one feature of our reality is in terms of the different structures which are implicit in different modes of interaction and which become explicit through legal ordering. The elucidation of their forms presupposes these interactions and could not proceed without them. The forms display the twofold intelligibility of interaction, and since form and content are epistemologically but not ontologically severable, the forms of interaction are as real as interaction itself.[37]

The point can also be put from the aspect of moral personality, which abstracts from particularity without dismissing it. It might be remarked that, strictly speaking, moral persons as such cannot interact. The purposiveness characteristic of moral personality is a purely inward quality, a mere potentiality that, so long as it remains potential, does not issue into the world and therefore does not act upon or interact with anything or anyone. In abstracting from all particularity, moral personality, it might be said, withdraws from the world and cannot leave its mark upon it. It is only through the realization of specific purposes that purposiveness radiates out from the actor and reaches his surroundings; the faculty of will impinges upon others only in so far as it wills something. All this is true. But far from undermining the significance of moral personality, this merely indicates how moral personality wins its way into the concreteness of interaction. Indeed it confirms the essentiality of moral personality by acknowledging that the rich variety of specific purposes is but the actualization of the potentiality of purposiveness. The intelligibility of private law reaches back through the content of particular purposes to the purposiveness which they express and achieve. The will, to be a will, must will something, but the particularity of what it wills does not confirm its status as a will but merely completes its operation. From the standpoint of corrective justice, purposiveness must issue into a particular purpose but into no purpose in particular. Corrective justice, then, does not deny particularity but treats it as a universal; it acknowledges that my purposiveness is complete only in *this* purpose, but the content of the purpose does not matter for it, since the "thisness" of this purpose refers to any and every purpose.[38]

The argument presented so far is a conceptual one about the nature

36 Plato, *Republic*, p. 509b.
37 In this respect the view being put forth here is consistent with the dictum of the great French Marxist, Alexandre Kojève, that "l'application de l'idée de Justice aux interactions sociales données n'est rien d'autre que le Droit" (*supra*, note 8, p. 319).
38 *Cf.* Hegel, *Phenomenology of Spirit*, para. 102.

and intelligibility of juridical relations. It points to an understanding of law through the forms of justice which render it intelligible, and it regards law in its positivity as the forum in which the indwelling and implicit intelligibility of external relations is realized and made explicit. In the set of relations for which the appropriate mode of understanding is corrective justice, law must be seen in non-instrumental terms and must mirror the non-instrumental quality of the transactions which it corrects. The structural features of the form of corrective justice place it conceptually beyond the reach of political determination and thereby vindicate the coherence of the notion of the Rule of Law in the context of the immediate relations which are the domain of private law.

The conceptual nature of this argument must be emphasized. Its focus is on intelligibility, not on desirability. It does not attend in the first instance to whether a specific legal relationship (or the law which governs it) is a good thing, but to what it is about which such a judgment might be invited. The priority of the attention to intelligibility is necessary because the evaluation of something is conceptually posterior to the understanding of what it is that is being evaluated. As the form of immediate interaction, corrective justice renders private law intelligible as what it is by disclosing the structure of transactions which private law orders and by contrasting the structure with that which marks distributions. The elucidation of the two categories of justice and of the interactions whose rationality they capture in no way implies that either is superior to the other. What is at stake is whether the non-instrumental conception of law, upon which the richest version of the Rule of Law depends, is a viable one. The relevance of corrective justice is that it is structurally immune to the instrumentalism which the Rule of Law denies, and that it thus shows how private law can be the initial configuration for juridical relationships conceived as the embodiment of the Rule of Law.

Indeed the question of desirability would be misplaced in view of the nature of the phenomenon whose intelligibility is sought. The complex of concepts with which this paper has concerned itself—the Rule of Law, private law, corrective justice, and moral personality—presents the central ingredients of a system of right which is self-sufficiently intelligible and therefore is not to be understood in instrumental terms. In other words, it presents the possibility that law might realize in a person's external relationships the internal freedom that characterizes him as a self-conscious, self-determining being. To demand of such a system of right that it justify itself in terms of some independent conception of the good is to fall into a category mistake. For the demand assumes that such a conception of the right must be valid only in so far as it promotes some extrinsically determined good which provides the ultimate ground of its intelligibility. But if this were so, it would not be the self-sufficiently intelligible and non-instrumental conception towards which the demand was addressed. This is confirmed by the grounding of the Rule of Law in moral personality. As the capacity for a conception of the good, moral personality is not itself a good but is an inescapable aspect of our existence as self-conscious beings. The hold which moral personality has upon us is not derived from our recognition of its desirability but from the actor's internal experience of its dynamic. The question appropriate to this account of the intelligibility of the Rule of Law is not whether this intelligibility is good but whether it is correct.

So far I have attempted to establish only the conceptual possibility of the Rule of Law. That possibility has been linked to other notions, such as the immediate ordering of interactions in corrective justice and the capacity for action in moral personality. In other words the Rule of Law has been presented, as Kant would put it, as "an idea of reason".[39] But such an idea "nonetheless has undoubted practical reality"[40] since it must be respected in the actualization of a legal system. The formal schema and the features within it which are pertinent to a non-instrumental conception of law thus represent only the starting point and not the entirety of a legal theory, which must go beyond the forms of justice to the integration of a content which adequately realizes these forms. Attention must be paid to the contours of specific legal doctrines against the background of their underlying forms, to the way in which the notion of positivity itself arises out of these forms, to the distinctive considerations which positivity introduces into the interplay of form and content, and to the way in which the non-instrumental features of the Rule of Law, which are so luminous in corrective justice, get carried over into the rest of the legal domain. Discussion of these matters, however, is for another occasion.[41]

---

39 Kant, "Theory and Practice" in *Kant's Political Writings*, ed. Reiss, p. 79.
40 *Ibid.*
41 A preliminary attempt to carry through the analysis to tort law appears in Weinrib, "Toward a Moral Theory of Negligence Law" (1983), 2 J. of Law and Philosophy 37.

The Political Theory of the Procedural Republic

Michael J. Sandel

My aim is to connect a certain debate in political theory with a certain development in our political practice. The debate is the one between rights-based liberalism and its communitarian, or civic republican critics. The development is the advent in the United States of what might be called the "procedural republic", a public life animated by the rights-based liberal ethic. In the modern American welfare state, it seems, the liberal dimensions of our tradition have crowded out the republican dimensions, with adverse consequences for the democratic prospect and the legitimacy of the regime.

In this paper, I will first identify the liberal and civic republican theories at issue in contemporary political philosophy, and then employ these contrasting theories in an interpretation of the American political condition. I hope ultimately to show that we can illuminate our political practice by identifying the contending political theories and self-images it embodies. This essay is a preliminary effort in that direction.

I

Liberals often take pride in defending what they oppose—pornography, for example, or unpopular views.[1] They say the state should not impose on its citizens a preferred way of life, but should leave them as free as possible to choose their own values and ends, consistent with a

---

1 In this and the following section, I draw on the introduction to Sandel, ed., *Liberalism and Its Critics* (Oxford: Basil Blackwell, 1984).

similar liberty for others. This commitment to freedom of choice requires liberals constantly to distinguish between permission and praise,
between allowing a practice and endorsing it. It is one thing to allow
pornography, they argue, something else to affirm it.

Conservatives sometimes exploit this distinction by ignoring it.
They charge that those who would allow abortions favour abortion, that
opponents of school prayer oppose prayer, that those who defend the
rights of Communists sympathize with their cause. And in a pattern of
argument familiar in our politics, liberals reply by invoking higher principles; it is not that they dislike pornography less, but rather that they
value toleration, or freedom of choice, or fair procedures more.

But in contemporary debate, the liberal rejoinder seems increasingly
fragile, its moral basis increasingly unclear. Why should toleration and
freedom of choice prevail when other important values are also at stake?
Too often the answer implies some version of moral relativism, the idea
that it is wrong to "legislate morality" because all morality is merely
subjective. "Who is to say what is literature and what is filth? That is a
value judgment, and whose values should decide?"

Relativism usually appears less as a claim than as a question. ("Who
is to judge?") But it is a question that can also be asked of the values
that liberals defend. Toleration and freedom and fairness are values too,
and they can hardly be defended by the claim that no values can be defended. So it is a mistake to affirm liberal values by arguing that all values
are merely subjective. The relativist defence of liberalism is no defence
at all.

What, then, can be the moral basis of the higher principles the liberal
invokes? Recent political philosophy has offered two main alternatives—
one utilitarian, the other Kantian. The utilitarian view, following John
Stuart Mill, defends liberal principles in the name of maximizing the general welfare. The state should not impose on its citizens a preferred way
of life, even for their own good, because doing so will reduce the sum
of human happiness, at least in the long run; better that people choose
for themselves, even if, on occasion, they get it wrong. "The only freedom which deserves the name," writes Mill, "is that of pursuing our
own good in our own way, so long as we do not attempt to deprive
others of theirs, or impede their efforts to obtain it." He adds that his
argument does not depend on any notion of abstract right, only on the
principle of the greatest good for the greatest number. "I regard utility
as the ultimate appeal on all ethical questions; but it must be utility in
the largest sense, grounded on the permanent interests of man as a progressive being."[2]

---

2 Mill, *On Liberty*, Ch. I.

Many objections have been raised against utilitarianism as a general doctrine of moral philosophy. Some have questioned the concept of utility, and the assumption that all human goods are in principle commensurable. Others have objected that by reducing all values to preferences and desires, utilitarians are unable to admit qualitative distinctions of worth, unable to distinguish noble desires from base ones. But most recent debate has focused on whether utilitarianism offers a convincing basis for liberal principles, including respect for individual rights.

In one respect, utilitarianism would seem well-suited to liberal purposes. Maximizing utility does not require judging people's values, only aggregating them. And the willingness to aggregate preferences without judging them suggests a tolerant spirit, even a democratic one. When people go to the polls, we count their votes whatever they are.

But the utilitarian calculus is not always as liberal as it first appears. If enough cheering Romans pack the Coliseum to watch the lion devour the Christian, the collective pleasure of the Romans will surely outweigh the pain of the Christian, intense though it be. Or if a big majority abhors a small religion and wants it banned, the balance of preferences will favour suppression, not toleration. Utilitarians sometimes defend individual rights on the grounds that respecting them now will serve utility in the long run. But this calculation is precarious and contingent. It hardly secures the liberal promise not to impose on some the values of others. As the majority will is an inadequate instrument of liberal politics—by itself it fails to secure individual rights—so the utilitarian philosophy is an inadequate foundation for liberal principles.

The case against utilitarianism was made most powerfully by Kant. He argued that empirical principles, such as utility, were unfit to serve as bases for the moral law. A wholly instrumental defense of freedom and rights not only leaves rights vulnerable, but fails to respect the inherent dignity of persons. The utilitarian calculus treats people as means to the happiness of others, not as ends in themselves, worthy of respect.[3]

Contemporary liberals extend Kant's argument with the claim that utilitarianism fails to take seriously the distinction between persons. In seeking above all to maximize the general welfare, the utilitarian treats society as a whole as if it were a single person; it conflates our many, diverse desires into a single system of desires, to be maximized. It is indifferent to the distribution of satisfactions among persons, except insofar as this may affect the overall sum. But this fails to respect our plur-

---

3 See Kant, *Groundwork of the Metaphysics of Morals* (1785; trans. H.J. Paton, New York: Harper and Row, 1956), and "On the Common Saying: 'This May be True In Theory, But It Does Not Apply in Practice,'" in Hans Reiss, ed., *Kant's Political Writings* (1793; Cambridge: Cambridge University Press, 1970).

ality and distinctness. It uses some as means to the happiness of all, and so fails to respect each as an end in himself.

Modern-day Kantians reject the utilitarian approach in favour of an ethic that takes rights more seriously. In their view, certain rights are so fundamental that even the general welfare cannot override them. As John Rawls writes,

> [e]ach person possesses an inviolability founded on justice that even the welfare of society as a whole cannot override. . . . the rights secured by justice are not subject to political bargaining or to the calculus of social interests.[4]

So Kantian liberals need an account of rights that does not depend on utilitarian considerations. More than this, they need an account that does not depend on any particular conception of the good, that does not presuppose the superiority of one way of life over others. Only a justification neutral about ends could preserve the liberal resolve not to favour any particular ends, or to impose on its citizens a preferred way of life.

But what sort of justification could this be? How is it possible to affirm certain liberties and rights as fundamental without embracing some vision of the good life, without endorsing some ends over others? It would seem we are back to the relativist predicament—to affirm liberal principles without embracing any particular ends.

The solution proposed by Kantian liberals is to draw a distinction between the "right" and the "good"—between a framework of basic rights and liberties, and the conceptions of the good that people may choose to pursue within the framework. It is one thing for the state to support a fair framework, they argue, something else to affirm some particular ends. For example, it is one thing to defend the right to free speech so that people may be free to form their own opinions and choose their own ends, but something else to support it on the grounds that a life of political discussion is inherently worthier than a life unconcerned with public affairs, or on the grounds that free speech will increase with general welfare. Only the first defense is available on the Kantian view, resting as it does on the ideal of a neutral framework.

Now the commitment to a framework neutral among ends can be seen as a kind of value—in this sense the Kantian liberal is no relativist— but its value consists precisely in its refusal to affirm a preferred way of life or conception of the good. For Kantian liberals, then, the right is prior to the good, and in two senses. First, individual rights cannot be

---

4 Rawls, *A Theory of Justice* (Oxford: Oxford University Press, 1971), pp. 3–4.

sacrificed for the sake of the general good, and second, the principles of justice that specify these rights cannot be premised on any particular vision of the good life. What justifies the rights is not that they maximize the general welfare or otherwise promote the good, but rather that they comprise a fair framework within which individuals and groups can choose their own values and ends, consistent with a similar liberty for others.

Of course, proponents of the rights-based ethic notoriously disagree about what rights are fundamental, and about what political arrangements the ideal of the neutral framework requires. Egalitarian liberals support the welfare state, and favour a scheme of civil liberties together with certain social and economic rights—rights to welfare, education, health care, and so on. Libertarian liberals defend the market economy, and claim that redistributive policies violate people's rights; they favour a scheme of civil liberties combined with a strict regime of private property rights. But whether egalitarian or libertarian, rights-based liberalism begins with the claim that we are separate, individual persons, each with our own aims, interests, and conceptions of the good, and seeks a framework of rights that will enable us to realize our capacity as free moral agents, consistent with a similar liberty for others.

II

Within academic philosophy, the last decade or so has seen the ascendance of the rights-based ethic over the utilitarian one, due in large part to the influence of John Rawls' important work, *A Theory of Justice*. In the debate between utilitarian and rights-based theories, the rights-based ethic has come to prevail. The legal philosopher H.L.A. Hart recently described the shift from

> the old faith that some form of utilitarianism must capture the essence of political morality to the new faith that the truth must lie with a doctrine of basic human rights, protecting specific basic liberties and interests of individuals. . . . Whereas not so long ago great energy and much ingenuity of many philosophers were devoted to making some form of utilitarianism work, latterly such energies and ingenuity have been devoted to the articulation of theories of basic rights.[5]

But in philosophy as in life, the new faith becomes the old or-

---

5 Hart, "Between Utility and Rights," in Alan Ryan, ed., *The Idea of Freedom* (Oxford: Oxford University Press, 1979), p. 77.

thodoxy before long. Even as it has come to prevail over its utilitarian rival, the rights-based ethic has recently faced a growing challenge from a different direction, from a view that gives fuller expression to the claims of citizenship and community than the liberal vision allows. Recalling the arguments of Hegel against Kant, the communitarian critics of modern liberalism question the claim for the priority of the right over the good, and the picture of the freely choosing individual it embodies. Following Aristotle, they argue that we cannot justify political arrangements without reference to common purposes and ends, and that we cannot conceive our personhood without reference to our role as citizens, and as participants in a common life.

This debate reflects two contrasting pictures of the self. The rights-based ethic, and the conception of the person it embodies, were shaped in large part in the encounter with utilitarianism. Where utilitarians conflate our many desires into a single system of desire, Kantians insist on the separateness of persons. Where the utilitarian self is simply defined as the sum of its desires, the Kantian self is a choosing self, independent of the desires and ends it may have at any moment. As Rawls writes, "The self is prior to the ends which are affirmed by it; even a dominant end must be chosen from among numerous possibilities."[6]

The priority of the self over its ends means I am never defined by my aims and attachments, but always capable of standing back to survey and assess and possibly to revise them. This is what it means to be a free and independent self, capable of choice. And this is the vision of the self that finds expression in the ideal of the state as a neutral framework. On the rights-based ethic, it is precisely because we are essentially separate, independent selves that we need a neutral framework, a framework of rights that refuses to choose among competing purposes and ends. If the self is prior to its ends, then the right must be prior to the good.

Communitarian critics of rights-based liberalism say we cannot conceive ourselves as independent in this way, as bearers of selves wholly detached from our aims and attachments. They say that certain of our roles are partly constitutive of the persons we are—as citizens of a country, or members of a movement, or partisans of a cause. But if we are partly defined by the communities we inhabit, then we must also be implicated in the purposes and ends characteristic of those communities. As Alasdair MacIntyre writes, "what is good for me has to be the good for one who inhabits these roles."[7] Open-ended though it be, the story

---

6 Rawls, *A Theory of Justice*, p. 560.

7 MacIntyre, *After Virtue* (Notre Dame: University of Notre Dame Press, 1981), p. 205.

of my life is always embedded in the story of those communities from which I derive my identity—whether family or city, people or nation, party or cause. On the communitarian view, these stories make a moral difference, not only a psychological one. They situate us in the world, and give our lives their moral particularity.

What is at stake for politics in the debate between unencumbered selves and situated ones? What are the practical differences between a politics of rights and a politics of the common good? On some issues, the two theories may produce different arguments for similar policies. For example, the civil rights movement of the 1960's might be justified by liberals in the name of human dignity and respect for persons, and by communitarians in the name of recognizing the full membership of fellow citizens wrongly excluded from the common life of the nation. And where liberals might support public education in hopes of equipping students to become autonomous individuals, capable of choosing their own ends and pursuing them effectively, communitarians might support public education in hopes of equipping students to become good citizens, capable of contributing meaningfully to public deliberations and pursuits.

On other issues, the two ethics might lead to different policies. Communitarians would be more likely than liberals to allow a town to ban pornographic bookstores, on the grounds that pornography offends its way of life and the values that sustain it. But a politics of civic virtue does not always part company with liberalism in favour of conservative policies. For example, communitarians would be more willing than some rights-oriented liberals to see states enact laws regulating plant closings, to protect their communities from the disruptive effects of capital mobility and sudden industrial change. More generally, where the liberal regards the expansion of individual rights and entitlements as unqualified moral and political progress, the communitarian is troubled by the tendency of liberal programs to displace politics from smaller forms of association to more comprehensive ones. Where libertarian liberals defend the private economy and egalitarian liberals defend the welfare state, communitarians worry about the concentration of power in both the corporate economy and the bureaucratic state, and the erosion of those intermediate forms of community that have at times sustained a more vital public life.

Liberals often argue that a politics of the common good, drawing as it must on particular loyalties, obligations, and traditions, opens the way to prejudice and intolerance. The modern nation-state is not the Athenian *polis*, they point out; the scale and diversity of modern life have rendered the Aristotelean political ethic nostalgic at best and dangerous at worst. Any attempt to govern by a vision of the good is likely to lead to a slippery slope of totalitarian temptations.

Communitarians reply that intolerance flourishes most where forms of life are dislocated, roots unsettled, traditions undone. In our day, the totalitarian impulse has sprung less from the convictions of confidently situated selves than from the confusions of atomized, dislocated, frustrated selves, at sea in a world where common meanings have lost their force. As Hannah Arendt has written, "What makes mass society so difficult to bear is not the number of people involved, or at least not primarily, but the fact that the world between them has lost its power to gather them together, to relate and to separate them."[8] Insofar as our public life has withered, our sense of common involvement diminished, we lie vulnerable to the mass politics of totalitarian solutions. So responds the party of the common good to the party of rights. If the party of the common good is right, our most pressing moral and political project is to revitalize those civic republican possibilities implicit in our tradition but fading in our time.

III

How might the contrast between the liberal and communitarian, or civic republican theories we have been considering help illuminate our present political condition? We might begin by locating these theories in the political history of the American republic. Both the liberal and the republican conceptions have been present throughout, but in differing measure and with shifting importance. Broadly speaking, the republican strand was most evident from the time of the founding to the late–19th century; by the mid– to late–20th century, the liberal conception came increasingly to predominate, gradually crowding out republican dimensions. I shall try in this section to identify three moments in the transition from the republican to the liberal constitutional order: (1) the civic republic; (2) the national republic; and (3) the procedural republic.

1. CIVIC REPUBLIC

The ideological origins of American politics is the subject of lively and voluminous debate among intellectual historians; some emphasize the Lockean liberal sources of American political thought, others the

---

8 Arendt, *The Human Condition* (Chicago: University of Chicago Press, 1958), pp. 52–53.

civic republican influences.[9] But beyond the question of who influenced the founders' thought is the further question of what kind of political life they actually lived. It is clear that the assumptions embodied in the practice of 18th century American politics, the ideas and institutions that together constitute the "civic republic", differ from those of the modern liberal political order in several respects. First, liberty in the civic republic was defined, not in opposition to democracy, as an individual's guarantee against what the majority might will, but as a function of democracy, of democratic institutions and dispersed power. In the 18th century, civil liberty referred not to a set of personal rights, in the sense of immunities, as in the modern "right to privacy", but, in Hamilton's words, "to a share in the government." Civil liberty was public, or political liberty, "equivalent to democracy or government by the people themselves." It was not primarily individual, but "the freedom of bodies politic, or States."[10]

Second, the terms of relation between the individual and the nation were not direct and unmediated, but indirect, mediated by decentralized forms of political association, participation, and allegiance. As Laurence Tribe points out, "it was largely through the preservation of boundaries between and among institutions that the rights of persons were to be secured."[11] Perhaps the most vivid constitutional expression of this fact is that the Bill of Rights did not apply to the states, and was not understood to create individual immunities from all government action. When Madison proposed, in 1789, a constitutional amendment providing that "no State shall infringe the equal rights of conscience, nor the freedom of speech or of the press, nor of the right of trial by jury in criminal cases," the liberal, rights-based ethic found its clearest early expression. But Madison's proposal was rejected by the Senate, and did not succeed until the 14th Amendment was passed some 79 years later.

Finally, the early republic was a place where the possibility of civic virtue was a live concern. Some saw civic virtue as essential to the preser-

---

9 For examples of the liberal view, see Louis Hartz, *The Liberal Tradition in America* (New York: Hartcourt Brace, 1955), and more recently, Isaac Kramnick, "Republican Revisionism Revisited," 87 *American Historical Review*, (1982), and John Diggins, *The Lost Soul of American Politics* (New York: Basic Books, 1984). For examples of the republican view, see Bernard Bailyn, *The Ideological Origins of the American Revolution* (Cambridge: Harvard University Press, 1967), Gordon Wood, *The Creation of the American Republic* (New York: Norton, 1969), and J.G.A. Pocock, *The Machiavellian Moment* (Princeton: Princeton University Press, 1975).

10 Wood, *The Creation of the American Republic*, pp. 24, 61.

11 Tribe, *American Constitutional Law* (Mineola: The Foundation Press, 1978), pp. 2–3.

vation of liberty; others despaired of virtue, and sought to design institutions that could function without it.[12] But as Tocqueville found in his visit to the New England townships, public life functioned in part as an education in citizenship:

> Town meetings are to liberty what primary schools are to science; they bring it within the people's reach, they teach men how to use and how to enjoy it. A nation may establish a free government, but without municipal institutions it cannot have the spirit of liberty.[13]

2. NATIONAL REPUBLIC

The transition to the national and, ultimately, the procedural republic, begins to unfold from the end of the Civil War to the turn of the century.[14] As national markets and large-scale enterprise displaced a decentralized economy, the decentralized political forms of the early republic became outmoded as well. If democracy was to survive, the concentration of economic power would have to be met by a similar concentration of political power. But the Progressives understood, or some of them did, that the success of democracy required more than the centralization of government; it also required the nationalization of politics. The primary form of political community had to be recast on a national scale. For Herbert Croly, writing in 1909, the "nationalizing of American political, economic, and social life" was "an essentially formative and enlightening political transformation." We would become more of a democracy only as we became "more of a nation . . . in ideas, in institutions, and in spirit."[15]

This nationalizing project would be consummated in the New Deal, but for the democratic tradition in America, the embrace of the nation was a decisive departure. From Jefferson to the populists, the party of democracy in American political debate had been, roughly speaking, the party of the provinces, of decentralized power, of small-town and small-scale America. And against them had stood the party of the nation—first Federalists, then Whigs, then the Republicans of Lincoln—a party that spoke for the consolidation of the union. It was thus the historic achieve-

---

12 See, for example, Madison, *Federalist*, No. 51, and Herbert Storing, *What the Anti-Federalists Were For* (Chicago: University of Chicago Press, 1981), Ch. 3.

13 Tocqueville, *Democracy in America*, vol. I, Ch. 5.

14 In this and the following section, I have drawn from Sandel, "The Procedural Republic and the Unencumbered Self," *Political Theory*, p. 12, (1984).

15 Croly, *The Promise of American Life* (Indianapolis: Bobbs-Merrill, 1965), pp. 270–73.

ment of the New Deal to unite, in a single party and political program, what Samuel Beer has called "liberalism and the national idea."[16]

What matters for our purpose is that, in the 20th century, liberalism made its peace with concentrated power. But it was understood at the start that the terms of this peace required a strong sense of national community, morally and politically to underwrite the extended involvements of a modern industrial order. If a virtuous republic of small-scale, democratic communities was no longer a possibility, a national republic seemed democracy's next best hope. This was still, in principle at least, a politics of the common good. It looked to the nation, not as a neutral framework for the play of competing interests, but rather as a formative community, concerned to shape a common life suited to the scale of modern social and economic forms.

But by the mid– or late–20th century, the national republic had run its course. Except for extraordinary moments, such as war, the nation proved too vast a scale across which to cultivate the shared self-understandings necessary to community in the formative, or constitutive sense. And yet, given the scale of economic and political life, there seemed no turning back. If so extended a republic could not sustain a politics of the common good, a different sort of legitimating ethic would have to be found. And so the gradual shift, in our practices and institutions, from a public philosophy of common purposes to one of fair procedures, from the national republic to the procedural republic.

3. PROCEDURAL REPUBLIC

The procedural republic represents the triumph of a liberal public philosophy over a republican one, with adverse consequences for democratic politics and the legitimacy of the regime. It reverses the terms of relation between liberty and democracy, transforms the relation of the individual and nation-state, and tends to undercut the kind of community on which it nonetheless depends. Liberty in the procedural republic is defined, not as a function of democracy but in opposition to democracy, as an individual's guarantee against what the majority might will. I am free insofar as I am the bearer of rights, where rights are trumps.[17] Unlike the liberty of the early republic, the modern version permits—in fact even requires—concentrated power. This has at least partly to do

---

16 Beer, "Liberalism and the National Idea," *The Public Interest*, Fall (1966), pp. 70–82.
17 See Ronald Dworkin, "Liberalism," in Stuart Hampshire, ed., *Public and Private Morality* (Cambridge: Cambridge University Press, 1978), p. 136.

with the universalizing logic of rights. Insofar as I have a right, whether to free speech or a minimum income, its provision cannot be left to the vagaries of local preferences but must be assured at the most comprehensive level of political association. It cannot be one thing in New York and another in Alabama. As rights and entitlements expand, politics is therefore displaced from smaller forms of association and relocated at the most universal form—in our case, the nation. And even as politics flows to the nation, power shifts away from democratic institutions (such as legislatures and political parties), toward institutions designed to be insulated from democratic pressures, and hence better equipped to dispense and defend individual rights (notably the judiciary and bureaucracy).

These institutional developments may begin to account for the sense of powerlessness that the welfare state fails to address and in some ways doubtless deepens. But it seems to me a further clue to our condition can be located in the vision of the unencumbered self that animates the liberal ethic. It is a striking feature of the welfare state that it offers a powerful promise of individual rights, and also demands of its citizens a high measure of mutual engagement. But the self-image that attends the rights cannot sustain the engagement. As bearers of rights, where rights are trumps, we think of ourselves as freely choosing, individual selves, unbound by obligations antecedent to rights, or to the agreements we make. And yet, as citizens of the procedural republic that secures these rights, we find ourselves implicated willy-nilly in a formidable array of dependencies and expectations we did not choose and increasingly reject.

In our public life, we are more entangled, but less attached, than ever before. It is as though the unencumbered self presupposed by the liberal ethic had begun to come true—less liberated than disempowered, entangled in a network of obligations and involvements unassociated with any act of will, and yet unmediated by those common identifications or expansive self-definitions that would make them tolerable. As the scale of social and political organization has become more comprehensive, the terms of our collective identity have become more fragmented, and the forms of political life have outrun the common purposes needed to sustain them.

Democracy and the Rule of Law

Allan C. Hutchinson and Patrick Monahan

The practice and theory of liberal democracy is in disarray. Condemned as utopian, ideals of full public participation and control have been pre-empted by an ethic of expertise. This contemporary orthodoxy holds that public policy should be formulated only by those properly qualified for the task; the role of the people is limited to choosing the elites who make the choices for them. The link between government policy and popular sentiment is, at best, obscure, with electoral apathy and disaffection the norm. For instance nearly a third of the Canadian electorate believe that politics either makes things worse or else has no effect in solving social problems.[1] In America, almost half the electorate does not vote in presidential elections. Public trust and confidence in government has fallen to the point where less than one-quarter of Americans believe that government is run for the "benefit of all".[2]

This is nothing new. There has never been a "golden age" of popular democracy except in the wishful thoughts of the nostalgic few. Thus the current apathy and elitism which dominates liberal democratic thinking lends scant support to critics who claim that present conditions constitute an exceptional crisis for democracy. Indeed, liberal democratic institutions have continually managed to confound critics, who have underestimated their resiliency and stamina. Representative democracy has flourished in the face of widespread citizen ennui precisely because public participation and interest are dispensable to its survival and performance. Limited public participation and apathy are even regarded in a positive

---

1 See J. Cohen and J. Rogers, *On Democracy; Toward a Transformation of American Society* (1983), pp. 32–35.
2 See H. Clarke et al., *Absent Mandate: The Politics of Discontent in Canada* (1984), pp. 32–33.

light, since they minimize conflict and promote stability. Democratic politics is seen as the legitimate preserve of specialists, whose only expertise happens to be that they have made a habit of engaging in political activity.

Whether by design or default, the courts have been proclaimed by many theorists as a proxy for a genuine democratic dialogue. The American Supreme Court has long been cast in the role of the nation's moral conscience. With the advent of an entrenched Charter of Rights and Freedoms in 1982, the Supreme Court of Canada is assuming a similar mantle. No longer seen merely as a means of constraining democratic debate and argument, courts act as elite forums for the enactment and resolution of this dialogue. Judicial review celebrates the triumph of detached philosophical deliberation over heated political haggling. Although a travesty of the democratic ideal, the judiciary's elevation to the status of moral prophet is defended and extolled by many in the name of democracy itself.[3]

Thomas Paine's assertion that "in America law is king" has never been more pertinent, not only in America but in Canada as well. Long a central feature of America's self-image, respect for the Rule of Law is becoming a vaunted article of Canadian constitutional faith. Indeed, the preamble to the Canadian Charter of Rights and Freedoms states that "Canada is founded upon principles that recognize the supremacy of God and the [R]ule of [L]aw." Law has been the gavel wielded to bring to order (or silence) competing voices in the cause of justice. In recent decades, the American Supreme Court has moved to front and centre on the political stage, intervening in heated political controversies. Paradoxically, the American Court's landmark decisions in *Brown* (desegregation) and *Roe v. Wade* (abortion) have worn very thin its claims to be acting within the bounds of constitutional propriety. Rising to the challenge, legal and political theorists have championed the relocation of political debate from the legislative crucible of communal controversy to the judicial "forum of principle". The judicialization of politics has been justified under the banner of the Rule of Law. Within this projected scenario, there is no conflict between an activist judiciary and democratic governance. Indeed, the Rule of Law is welcomed as a necessary component of a properly functioning democratic polity. Checking popular excesses, litigation is thought to provide a privileged occasion for the renewal of society's commitment to continuing moral discourse.

---

3 See, for example, M. Perry, *The Constitution, The Courts and Human Rights: An Inquiry into the Legitimacy of Constitutional Policymaking by the Judiciary* (1982), pp. 91–145.

Notwithstanding recent valiant attempts to reconcile the Rule of Law with democratic theory, this gambit fails. The Rule of Law functions as a clear check on the flourishing of a rigorous democracy. Attempts to characterize the Rule of Law as the butler of democracy are false and misleading. Liberal legalism is premised on the same logic of expertise which has made popular control over public policy dispensable. It is simply more evidence of the demise of contestability as the touchstone of politics. The first part of the essay will trace the historical and theoretical connections between the Rule of Law and liberal democracy. The second part will offer a more searching criticism of the elite and marginal practice of constitutional adjudication. The final section reasserts the primacy of democratic over legalistic values and seeks to sketch a practical vision of democratic practice.

1. THE BRIDLE OF POWER: LAW AND POLITICS

(a) Liberalism, Law and Democracy

The sonorous and majestic ring of the appeal to the Rule of Law has resonated through the centuries. It has operated as a potent call to moral arms, a clarion-call for constitutional justice by a whole host of political actors and combatants. At times, the Rule of Law has been used to legitimize and galvanize a challenge to entrenched power; at others, the ruling elite has relied upon it to sanction its power and resistance to would-be usurpers. Like any ideal, it only exists in the political consciousness and conscience. But, like every other ideal, it exercises a tenacious grip on the imagination and actions of its adherents. Indeed, its ideological attraction and political durability are largely attributable to its historical plasticity, the facility to accommodate itself to changing governmental situations and political forces. In short, it is the will-o'-the-wisp of constitutional history.

Notwithstanding its protean nature, the rich historical tapestry of the Rule of Law has been loosely connected by a strong liberal thread: it has been used as a seductive slogan in the struggle to establish or preserve individual liberty and action. On many occasions, this appeal to liberty has amounted to nothing more than moralistic window-dressing for otherwise naked attempts to seize political power, a rhetorical gambit in a continuing power-play. But to reduce the appeal to the Rule of Law to simply and always an exercise in mystification is to distort the historical record; it impugns the honourable motives of many and overestimates the credulity of even more.[4] Over the last millenium, the Rule of

---

4 See, for example, *E.P. Thompson, Whigs and Hunters* (1975).

Law has occasionally proved to be an effective principle to check the indulgent abuse of power by the few over the many. However, over the long haul, the Rule of Law has been activated as a "principled" counter in the shuffling of power among elite groups; it has served to inhibit the flourishing of any governmental system of direct democracy.

The Rule of Law is more concerned with and committed to individual liberty than democratic governance. The historical development of any kind of democracy has been the by-product of a preoccupation with private autonomy. The Rule of Law is premised on the ideal of limited government; it has stood as a constitutional barrier between the governors and the governed, between power and people. The existence and extent of democratic governance is only justified insofar as it better serves the enhanced liberty of individuals; it is a recent recruit on the proclaimed march to the truly liberal state. Indeed, universal suffrage is a decidedly twentieth century phenomenon. Even today, representative democracy only extends to about 20 per cent of the world's nations (not population) and, in many of these states, the arrangements are extremely fragile and incomplete.

The compulsion to reason within a closed system of premises is said to guarantee the enduring integrity and efficacy of the constitutional compact and insulate the judges from ideological controversy. Within this constitutional scenario, adherence to the Rule of Law has come to be synonymous with compliance with a liberal scheme of constitutional governance. Although some form of representative democracy has become a modern component of this model, the history of the Rule of Law's theory and practice reveals that it is more an optional extra than an essential condition. Indeed, the opposite often seems to be true: the Rule of Law has functioned as a clear check on the actual impact and expansion of a rigorous democracy.

(b) The Thick and the Thin

If not non-democratic in aspiration and orientation, the Rule of Law is democratically indifferent in character and scope. The enduring concerns of the Rule of Law are the limitation of state power, the maintenance of a broad sphere of private liberty and the preservation of a market-exchange economy. In its many academic manifestations, it has been connected, to greater and lesser extents, to an individualistic theory of political justice and jurisprudence. Ostensibly, there have been two versions of the Rule of Law, but they both represent a commitment to liberalism; it is simply that one tends to be more explicit and marked than the other.

The "thin" version of the Rule of Law amounts to a constitutional principle of legality. It demands that government be conducted in accordance with established and performable norms; its voice remains silent or, at best, whispered on the issue of substantive policies. Rule must be by law and not discretion. Also, and especially, the lawmaker itself must be under the law, at least until it changes the law. In this "thin" form, the Rule of Law is targeted against arbitrary government and palm-tree justice. Its critical logo is "a government of laws, not men"; its operative axioms are the generality of official rules and the faithful adherence by government to those declared standards of conduct. The modern defence of such a "thin" version is that the preferred system of governance is that in which "the law furnishes a base-line for self-directed action, not a detailed set of instructions for accomplishing specific objectives."[5]

Although far from explicit or necessarily so, its substantive tendency is clearly toward a liberal society in which the best government is the one which governs least. However, unless such a constitutional requirement of official legality is supplemented by a "thicker" theory of political justice, the Rule of Law will be a weak restraint on an ambitiously unjust regime. It might even tend to legitimate its substantive excesses under a patina of formal justice. Unrepresentative government and the Rule of Law are not mutually exclusive; democracy is an entirely dispensable feature of this form of the Rule of Law. As Herbert Hart has observed, "however great the aura of majesty or authority which the official system may have, its demands in the end must be submitted to moral scrutiny."[6] Accordingly, a full and proper defence and understanding of the Rule of Law must be based on its foundational and substantive political connections.

The "thick" version of the Rule of Law incorporates the thinner one as merely one dimension of a liberal theory of justice. This conception of the Rule of Law goes back to the Greeks and Romans, but finds its modern roots in the Enlightenment.[7] Indeed, there is an almost direct line of descent from the theory and practice of 17th century England to that of late 20th century Anglo-America. The intellectual lineage runs almost unbroken from John Locke and Thomas Hobbes to John Rawls and Ronald Dworkin, through Thomas Paine, John Stuart Mill, A.V. Dicey and Friedrich Hayek. The modern defence of this "thick" version posits

---

5 L. Fuller, *The Morality of Law* (rev. ed., 1969), p. 210.

6 H.L.A. Hart, *The Concept of Law* (1961), p. 206.

7 For an historical introduction to these events, see H. Berman, *Law and Revolution: The Formation of the Western Legal Tradition* (1983).

the necessary connection between procedural and substantive justice. The Rule of Law demands that positive law embody a particular vision of social justice, structured around the moral rights and duties which citizens have against each other and the state as a whole.

(c) 1215 And All That

Modern scholarship and constitutional practice can be traced back to the Glorious Revolution and, even beyond that, to the Magna Carta. Before the 17th century, increased individual liberty was more an incidental cost of the political struggle than the result of any deliberate strategy. Beginning with the Magna Carta in 1215, the barons sought to restrain the monarchical monopoly by demanding that the sovereign act only *per legem terrae*. And, as early as the 13th century, jurists like Henry de Bracton argued that even the king was *sub Deo et lege*; "law is the bridle of power."[8] However, by the 15th century at latest, the Magna Carta had become an obscure and hollow proclamation, only later to be romanticised by some modern legal historians. It was not until after the Tudor Reformation, when the Stuarts sought to re-invoke the divine right of kings, that the Rule of Law came into its own as an influential and effective piece of constitutional rhetoric for curbing royal power. Within this encounter, the idea and establishment of some democratic dimension to political governance was of little consequence or concern.[9]

1610 was a banner year for the Rule of Law. Sir Edward Coke, later to be dismissed as Chief Justice and become a parliamentarian committed to reviving the memory of the Magna Carta as the great charter of English freedom, held in *Dr. Bonham's Case* that "the Common Law will controll Acts of Parliament, and sometimes adjudge them to be utterly void."[10] Also, in that year, the House of Commons presented James I with the Petition of Grievances, insisting that he continue the tradition of being "guided and governed by certain rule of law." Matters did not come to a head until 1625 when Charles I assumed the throne. As so often, the major bone of contention was the right to levy taxes. The price for Parliament's compliance with Charles' fiscal demands was royal assent to the Petition of Right. This enacted that the king would govern

---

8 *On The Laws and Customs of England*, vol. 2 (S. Thorne trans., 1968), p. 305.

9 For an accessible and informed account of this history, see J. Ridley, *The History of England* (1981) and E. Schnapper, "The Parliament of Wonders" (1984), 83 Colum. L. Rev. 1665.

10 (1610), 77 E.R. 638, 652.

according to the laws and statutes of the realm; that no one could be arrested by the king's order, but only for the breach of a specific offence; that only Parliament could impose taxes; and that civilians could not be made subject to martial law.

It must not be forgotten that, although these events have been regarded by generations of constitutional lawyers as laying the foundations for the modern Rule of Law, they were motivated more by a revolutionary than a legal spirit. Nevertheless, they did establish that henceforth law was the "instrument and prize; he who would control the constitution would have first to control the law."[11] But, importantly, it has to be added that Parliament did not embark on this course of action as part of a campaign to transfer power to the general populace; the progressive tenor of the times was resoundingly libertarian and not democratic.

For the next two centuries, the English constitution remained a pragmatic melange of monarchical, aristocratic and democratic ingredients, bound together by a strong libertarian commitment. Yet, the half century after 1628 demonstrated an important historical lesson that many societies, including our own, continue to overlook: a law is worth little more than the paper it is written on unless it is accompanied by sufficient willingness *and power* to translate its promises into practice. Indeed, after the Petition of Right, Charles almost immediately dissolved Parliament and ruled alone for 11 years. Although Parliament was briefly recalled, England was soon riven by Civil War. The country was not returned to some semblance of normality until the Glorious Revolution of 1688. Significantly, the monarchy was restored, but only on terms laid down by Parliament.

A major instrument of government and statement of political intent was the Bill of Rights. While this is the closest England has ever come to adopting a written constitution, it was never more than another piece of legislation, repealable by any later Parliament. The central thrust of the legislation was to force the Crown to rule through Parliament. Its constitutional ambition was not to popularize government, but to restore and conserve "the true auntient and indubitable rights and liberties of the people." It dispensed with the Stuarts' extravagant claims to rule by prerogative writ, ensuring that every parliamentarian had freedom of speech and that "cruel and unusual punishments" were prohibited. These provisions were supplemented by the Act of Settlement in 1701; a major clause was that judges no longer held office at the king's whim, but *quamdiu se bene gesserint* (during good behaviour).

---

11 H. Nenner, *By Colour of Law* (1977), p. xi.

The undisputed apologist for these constitutional developments was John Locke, the father of modern liberalism. In his *Second Treatise on Government*, he provided the enduring account of how people created civil society to protect better their individual rights enjoyed in a state of nature. Within such a constitutional scheme, the limited role of government was to enact law "as guards and fences to the properties of all the members of society." The Rule of Law was a pivotal principle. Laws were to be general in scope and operation; "freedom of men under government is . . . not to be subject to the inconstant, unknown, arbitrary will of another man." While Locke justified the initial success, it was 18th century writers, like David Hume, Edmund Burke and William Paley, who consolidated the constitutional position of the Rule of Law. Yet, it was the Americans who were to embrace and implement most directly the Lockean teachings.

(d) The American Experiment

Although England had proceeded on the path to parliamentary supremacy, the American colonists were more inclined to resuscitate the Magna Carta and its libertarian underpinnings against a recalcitrant English Parliament. After the Revolution, America set about establishing its own constitutional order. Despite significant divisions, the preferred basis for republican government was not democracy. While, by existing standards, America was enviably more representative in governance than most nations, the Founders' rabid libertarianism was only matched by its faint-hearted commitment to popular rule. As one prominent Philadelphia Conventioneer, Elbridge Gerry, put it, "the evils we experience flow from the excess of democracy."[12] People's supposed natural rights were to be put beyond the imagined vicissitudes of majoritarian politics. In particular, private property was not to be open to governmental interference. After all, the War of Independence had been fought over this very principle. The relation between personal liberty and popular democracy has been neatly described by Martin Diamond:

---

12 *The Records of the Federal Convention of 1787*, vol. 1, ed. M. Farrand (1937), p. 48. Roger Sherman's response was to the democratic point. Bills of Rights were "mere paper protection"; "the only real security that you can have for all your important rights must be in the nature of your government. . . . If you are about to trust your liberties with people whom it is necessary to bind by stipulation . . . your stipulation is not even worth the trouble of writing." "Letters of a Countryman, November 22, 1787", reprinted in *Essays on the Constitution of the United States*, ed. P. Ford (1910), p. 220.

. . . .for the founding generation it was liberty that was the comprehensive good, the end against which political things had to be measured; and democracy was only a form of government which, like any other form of government, had to prove itself adequately instrumental to the security of liberty.[13]

This liberal theory of democracy has continued to dominate American constitutional life. In effect, the American Revolution only managed to replace the dominion of a foreign power with that of a domestic document.[14] Entrenched individual rights always trump any collective concerns of the democratic process. Enforcing this social compact, the courts were to function as the guardians of the Rule of Law. But, in the process, they were not to turn themselves into an independent centre of constitutional power. As John Marshall announced, "judicial power, as contradistinguished from the power of laws, has no existence. Courts are the mere instruments of the law, and can will nothing."[15] The Rule of Law demanded a scrupulously objective and formalistic judiciary.

While the upholding of the Rule of Law in the United States was being increasingly entrusted to the judicial interpreters of the written constitution, the English constitution remained proudly and defiantly unwritten. Indeed, A.V. Dicey maintained that the Constitution is not "the source, but the consequence of the rights of individuals."[16] Writing at the dusk of the Victorian laissez-faire era and at pains to check the runaway development of a collectivistically-inclined bureaucracy, he symbolized the modern attempt to reinvigorate the Rule of Law as a set of constitutional postulates devoted to safeguarding individual interests and liberty. Dicey's Rule of Law comprised "three distinct though kindred conceptions."[17]: no one can be punished except for a breach of the ordinary law, established in the ordinary legal manner before the ordinary courts; no one is above the law and everyone, especially officials, is amenable to the ordinary law; and the general principles of the constitution, protecting private rights, are the result of the ordinary laws. The combined force and design of Dicey's principles was to make the Rule of Law into a bridle for a supposedly rampant administrative arm of government.

---

13 "The Declaration and The Constitution: Liberty, Democracy and The Founders" in *The American Commonwealth*, ed. N. Glazer (1976), p. 47.

14 See E. Corwin, *The "Higher Law" Background of American Constitutional Law* (1965).

15 *Osborn v. Bank of the United States*, 22 U.S. 738, 866 (1824).

16 *The Law of the Constitution* (1885), p. 46. Reference will be made to the 10th ed., E. Wade (1965).

17 *Ibid.*, at 188–203.

The Diceyian tradition of Lockean conservatism has been continued by Friedrich Hayek in the contemporary debate over the Rule of Law. For him, the Rule of Law stands in unequivocal opposition to state redistribution and planning; it is the essential and most important condition of individual freedom.[18] It is not simply a constitutional principle of "legality", but comprises a substantive vision of the correct and just relations between individuals and society:

> Nothing distinguishes more clearly conditions in a free country from those in a country under arbitrary government than the observance in the former of the great principles known as the [R]ule of [L]aw. Stripped of all technicalities this means that government in all its actions is bound by rules fixed and announced beforehand—rules which make it possible to see with fair certainty how the authority will use its coercive powers in given circumstances, and to plan one's individual affairs on the basis of this knowledge.[19]

Not surprisingly, Hayek identifies the inter-war years, culminating in the New Deal, as the period when America began to renege on its original constitutional compact and to subvert the Rule of Law. For him, an activist government, let alone an activist judiciary, is anathema to the Rule of Law and its libertarian foundations.

This tradition has been continued by contemporary writers. Although the emphasis has become more liberal than libertarian, democracy remains very much a secondary feature of the constitutional order. Most writers agree that the Rule of Law is a vital protective and facilitative constitutional device for a fundamental scheme of individual rights; disagreement is over the scope and character of those rights. In this sense, the protean quality of the Rule of Law has allowed it to be extended beyond civil and political rights to social and economic entitlements without sacrificing its essential nature. The product of a multi-national conference, the Declaration of Delhi in 1958 stated that the Rule of Law is, apart from its traditional concerns, intended "to establish social, economic, educational and cultural conditions under which [individuals'] legitimate aspirations and dignity may be realized."[20]

(d)   The Contemporary Debate: Democratizing The Rule of Law

The work of Ronald Dworkin, temporarily at least, dominates the animated contemporary debate over the judicial role under the Rule of

---

18   See *The Constitution of Liberty* (1960) and *The Political Ideal of the Rule of Law* (1955).
19   *The Road To Serfdom* (1946), p. 54.
20   International Commission of Jurists, The Rule of Law in a Free Society (1959), p. 3.

Law. Adjudication is claimed to satisfy the Rule of Law by meeting the democratic demand for judicial objectivity and the popular need for political equity. While some rail that an activist judiciary is antithetical to democratic governance,[21] Dworkin argues that, if judges are to fulfil their democratic responsibilities under the Rule of Law, they must make political decisions, albeit not personal or partisan ones. His claim is bold and brilliant. The traditional formalistic, rule-book conception of the Rule of Law requires judges in hard cases to be unconstrainedly creative or to dissemble. Dworkin's rights conception of the Rule of Law incorporates a dimension of substantive fairness and thereby appropriately constrains and guides the judge in the resolution of hard cases. In defending such a version of the Rule of Law, Dworkin keeps himself firmly within the tradition of Locke and the constitutional priority of liberty; "the idea of individual rights . . . is the zodiac sign under which America was born."[22]

For Dworkin, judges are political actors whose power is limited by a legal system's history and its liberal character. The state does not give them a blank check on which to write in the political currency of their choice; they must interpret the regnant legal materials in their best light as a theory of political morality. The judge breathes political vitality into the lifeless words of legal texts by applying the twin tests of "formal fit" and "substantive justice". Any interpretation must be able to demonstrate some plausible connection with society's legal history. However, the better theory is not necessarily the one that accounts for the most decisions or statutes; "formal fit" is only a heuristic device or rule-of-thumb. This requirement acts as a threshold and combines with the test of "substantive justice". This obliges the judge to develop a scheme of rights which a just state would establish and enforce. While this task can only be provisionally and partially performed, the conscious striving for such a perfected theory is the hallmark of adjudication under the Dworkinian conception of the Rule of Law. Accordingly, judicial power is legitimated by this commitment to uphold the existing political order of rights and only to extend it in a consistent and principled manner. In this way, law is and remains rational, just and objective.

It is to Dworkin's credit that he does not disguise his individualistic revitalization of the Rule of Law. He openly concedes that his conception

---

21 See John Hart Ely, *Democracy and Distrust* (1980), p. 67 ("we may rant until we're blue in the face that legislatures aren't wholly democratic, but that isn't going to make courts more democratic than legislatures").

22 R. Dworkin, "Political Judges and the Rule of Law" in *A Matter of Principle* (1985), p. 31.

might well exact a price in the development of a communitarian spirit. Yet, anxious to deflect charges of being insufficiently democratic, he reminds us that his conception of the Rule of Law "enriches democracy by adding an independent forum of principle . . . [where] justice is in the end a matter of individual right, and not independently a matter of the public good."[23] He casts the Supreme Court as the central constitutional institution through which the citizenry can debate, articulate and implement its collective standards for social justice. Dworkin is not alone in elevating legal conversation to a privileged form of democratic discourse. Joined by other writers, like Owen Fiss and Laurence Tribe, Bruce Ackerman has gone so far as to suggest that:

> Not that a vigorous and constructive legal dialogue can ever hope to compensate for an apathetic and muddled political debate. Yet the reverse is also true: political commitment is no substitute for legal deliberation. While the future of America depends on the American people, the future of American law depends, in a special way, on the way American lawyers interpret their calling.[24]

2. DEMOCRATIC INDIVIDUALISM AND THE RULE OF LAW

(a) Democracy and Community

Liberalism has always been ambivalent about the significance and the desirability of the value of community. For liberal theory, all roads begin with atomic, prepolitical individuals maximizing their self-interest. Thus, social contract theorists like Hobbes and Locke justified the creation of the state by analogy to a self-interested bargain between autonomous individuals in a state of nature. There was little emphasis on the possibility of the state helping to forge communal values or common ends. The state was necessary merely as a means of establishing order in a universe in which the interests of rational maximizers inevitably collided with each other.[25] The order that resulted was always in possible jeopardy, since it depended on a delicate and even-handed resort to carrots and sticks.

This emphasis on the self-interested and autonomous individual receives its highest and most explicit expression in contemporary theories

---

23 *Ibid.*, at p. 32. In his most recent book, Dworkin develops and elaborates on these themes and emphasizes that the Rule of Law is "the parent and guardian of democracy." See *Law's Empire* (1986), p. 399.

24 *Reconstructing American Law* (1984), p. 110.

25 See generally, C.B. Macpherson, *The Life and Times of Liberal Democracy* (1977) and *Democratic Theory: Essays in Retrieval* (1973).

of democratic institutions and behaviour. Current analyses of "polyarchal" forms of democracy lack any genuine conception of public, communal values. Democracy is simply a mechanism for choosing governments in which sets of elites compete for the right to rule. According to some observers, there is no necessary connection between the choices made by the elites and the desires of the electorate. Instead, the elites themselves formulate and resolve the issues. The demands of the voters are not the ultimate data of the system since these demands are themselves shaped or manufactured; the public's demand for political goods "does not flow from its initiative but is being shaped, and the shaping of it is an essential part of the democratic process."[26]

Other analyses of democracy do not adopt such an impoverished conception of the community and its values. Yet even when the volitions of the electorate are seen as independent rather than manufactured, the analysis continues to be framed in market terms. Individual consumers "spend" their votes so as to maximize their individual self-interest, rather than to further the ends of the community as a whole. In fact, the invocation of the "public interest" is simply an ideological masquerade for the aggregation of private interests. Citizenship involves striking bargains in one's own interest rather than forging and debating the fundamental values of the community.[27]

Polyarchal forms of democracy reinforce the very consumer mentality they purport to serve. Because effective decision-making occurs at the elite rather than the mass level, the average citizen assumes no responsibility for shaping the values, beliefs and actions of the community. Even the act of voting, the one form of citizen participation which is sanctioned and encouraged, is a jealously guarded private activity; there is no necessity for individuals to discuss or justify their choices to others.[28] In polyarchical politics, spectacle has eclipsed substance. Given an electorate unaccustomed to participating in meaningful debate over

---

26 Schumpeter, *Capitalism, Socialism and Democracy* (1943), p. 282. For a useful discussion of the extent to which volitions of citizens are constrained in liberal democracies, see Lindblom, *Politics and Markets* (1977), pp. 208–213.

27 For examples of this economic and interest group theory of democracy, see Anthony Downs, *An Economic Theory of Democracy* (1957); Mancur Olson Jr., *The Logic of Collective Action* (1965); Robert Dahl, *Dilemmas of Pluralist Democracy: Autonomy Versus Control* (1982).

28 ". . . our primary electoral act, voting, is rather like using a public toilet: we wait in line with a crowd in order to close ourselves up in a small compartment where we can relieve ourselves in solitude and in privacy of our burden, pull a lever, and then, yielding to the next in line, go silently home." B. Barber, *Direct Democracy* (1984), p. 188.

public values, election campaigns have become prized occasions for the marketing of "leadership" rather than informed discussion and choice by citizens. To the extent that issues are discussed at all, they are framed in such abstract terms (for example, "inflation" or "the deficit") as to be virtually unintelligible and have only ephemeral impact on voter choice.[29] The stunted character of this public discourse on values calls to mind Rousseau's dictum that without informed and active citizens, you have nothing but "debased slaves, from the rulers of the state downwards."[30]

The great challenge for modern democratic theory has been to justify this elitist version of democratic practice. Most justifications centre on the "realism" of representative forms of democracy. Since citizens are largely apathetic about public affairs; it is thought to be appropriate that decision-making be left to the discretion of representative elites. It is considered utopian to require all issues of public policy to be submitted for electoral debate and decision.

Notions of law and legality have played a subsidiary but significant role in the justification of polyarchal forms of democracy. Adherents to the "thick" Rule of Law have suggested that there is no necessary tension between their proposals and democratic decision-making; the Rule of Law has an important role to play in tempering and modifying the elitism in modern liberal democracies.

This might be accomplished in a variety of ways. On one view, the Rule of Law serves as a guarantee to individuals that their rights will not be ignored by the bureaucracies of the state, the corporation or the trade union. The Rule of Law requires that fundamental issues of political morality be debated as issues of principle and not simply issues of political power. The positive effects of judicial review are thought to extend far beyond the particular case or dispute before a court. The claim is that "rights talk" is a means of uplifting and revitalizing political and moral discourse in our society generally. By forcing the political process to confront the question of individual rights, public morality will become more reflective and self-critical.[31] Cast as the high priests of moral discourse,

---

29 For instance, a recent analysis of voter attitudes in Canada found that issues which were seen as central in the 1974 election were barely mentioned in the 1979 campaign. When a third election was held some nine months later in 1980, a whole new set of concerns was seen as central. The shifts in public perceptions were closely related to the agenda of discussion set by the media and the political leaders. See Clarke, *supra*, note 2 at pp. 77–99.

30 J.J. Rousseau, "A Discourse on Political Economy" in *Social Contract and Discourses*, p. 251.

31 For arguments to this effect see Ackerman, *supra*, note 24.

the judiciary encourages and orchestrates meaningful public debate on moral issues.

These claims that the Rule of Law can serve as an indispensable means of popular control are profoundly mistaken. The Rule of Law sustains elitist politics, with its impoverished sense of community. It does so in at least two related, but distinct ways. First, the Rule of Law's language of rights reinforces the assumption that communities are nothing more than aggregations of private interests. Rightholders are defined in contradistinction to the community rather than as integral components of it. Second, and more significantly, a politics dominated by the Rule of Law is a politics with limited scope for popular participation and control. It cramps and compresses the ability of individuals to debate and define the conditions of their communal life. In attempting to avoid the tyranny of the majority, it mistakenly embraces a doctrine of expertise and dependency which carries with it a subtle, yet despotic dominion of its own.

(b) Citizens as Rightholders

Democratic politics is not guaranteed to produce "right answers". No matter how much debate and discussion is encouraged or exists, there is still the possibility that the community will make a choice that is mean-spirited or unenlightened. This is implicit in democratic politics. A choice for democracy means that the community has a right to be wrong. Even if a citizen vehemently disagrees with a particular democratic outcome, that outcome is still entitled to a measure of respect simply by virtue of the fact that it embodies the democratic will of the community.

The notion that decisions that are "wrong" should nevertheless be entitled to respect may seem paradoxical or unsettling.[32] Consider a case where a citizen believed not only that the community's decision was wrong-headed, but that the error could be demonstrated through appeal to an uncontroversial or "neutral" form of reasoning. In such a case, that person might find it particularly galling if the collective decision were permitted to stand. He or she might struggle to discover some way of maintaining a general commitment to democracy, while disavowing the legitimacy of the community's choice on this particular occasion.

---

32 See, for example, R. Wollheim, "A Paradox in the Theory of Democracy", in P. Laslett and W.G. Runciman, eds., *Philosophy, Politics and Society* (2nd Series, 1962), pp. 71–87.

In essence, this is the attitude of those theorists who accord a central, primary role to considerations of legality and constitutionalism. Defenders of the Rule of Law do not deny that the democratic community has the right to be wrong. They simply contend that this prerogative exists within a closely circumscribed sphere. If the democratic community strays outside its appointed area and trespasses onto prohibited turf, the appropriate response is self-evident: like antibodies attacking a foreign substance, the judiciary should move swiftly to excise the offending contagion before it spreads uncontrollably throughout the body politic.

Of course, the perennial difficulty is to define the alleged boundaries of democratic politics. Contemporary political philosophy claims to have noticed these boundaries lurking in the interstices of Kantian moral theory. The argument runs a typical course.[33] Individuals are entitled to be treated as ends in themselves, rather than as a means to someone else's ends. In order to give effect to this background political ideal, it is necessary to specify the conditions under which each individual's qualities of moral agency and personality are recognized. These political conditions form a coherent whole. They can be expressed in the form of a series of entitlements or rights which must be respected by the community if it is to be true to the notion of individual autonomy. A community cannot be said to be just or rightly ordered until and unless it recognizes and guarantees these individual rights. Such a schema represents the fixed fulcrum around which democratic politics must swing.

Although this rights theory purports to leave basic democratic principles intact, it frustrates and paralyzes them. This results as much from what is excluded as included in the theory. Significantly, a rights-based conception of the Rule of Law has an impoverished or non-existent conception of communal politics. There is very little respect and a good deal of anxiety surrounding attempts on the part of the community to define its collective identity. For the rights theorist, wherever collectivities gather together to express their moral beliefs in law, there lurks the stale, but unmistakable whiff of totalitarianism on the political breeze. Questions of morality and values are considered to be inescapably relative. Such matters of taste must be left in the hands of individuals, freed from the tyranny of the opinions of others regarding their lifestyles.

The constitutional analysis of Ronald Dworkin exemplifies this impoverished conception of community with its corresponding emphasis

---

33 For instances of the line of argument described in this paragraph, see J. Rawls, *A Theory of Justice* (1971); and R. Nozick, *Anarchy, State, and Utopia* (1974).

on the privatization of morality.[34] Dworkin's analysis is premised on the notion that everyone has the right to be treated with equal concern and respect. This concern for equality is violated when the community allows a "corrupting" element to contaminate its calculation of general welfare. The corrupting element can be identified on the basis of a distinction between personal and external preferences. Individuals' personal preferences relate to the assignment of goods or advantages to themselves, while external preferences relate to the assignment of goods or advantages to others. According to Dworkin, a utilitarianism that counts both personal and external preferences is vulgar and corrupt. External preferences do not respect the right of everyone to be treated with equal concern and respect; they suppose that a particular form of life or community is more valuable than any other. For instance, to take one of Dworkin's examples, if there is a proposal to build a swimming pool, only the votes of those who want to use the pool may properly be counted in its favour. Non-swimmers who might support the construction of the pool because they wish to promote the activity of swimming should be ignored. This is because the non-swimmers are suggesting that a certain lifestyle or activity is inherently more valuable than another.

Far from purifying utilitarian discourse, Dworkin's proposal debases it. In the guise of offering a political discourse that is neutral and egalitarian, Dworkin has simply ordained that only certain values or ideals may be tolerated in political debate and argument. The accepted ideolect is that employed by individuals bargaining in their own self interest. They are entitled to be heard only if they frame their claims in terms of what they hope to gain personally from a decision. Any appeal to the values or interests of the community as a whole is corrupting. Apparently, to invoke public as opposed to private considerations is to violate the norm of equal concern and respect.

Dworkin exhibits a profound antipathy for common consciousness amongst citizens. Politics becomes nothing more than a lackey for private interest. Pluralism and relativism are constitutionally mandated because there can be no genuine public interests. The result is an aggregate of individuals secure in their abstract rights and liberties but divorced from each other. This, of course, is entirely predictable given the background theory of personality which underlies contemporary liberal accounts of politics. The common starting point of these accounts is a fictitious choosing self, stripped of all particularity. This abstract self be-

---

34 See R. Dworkin, *Taking Rights Seriously* (1977).

longs to no particular family or community, has no set of allegiances or commitments and possesses no life plan. Although liberalism fetes the individual and celebrates personal freedom, it recommends a set of social organizing principles that rests on a pessimistic notion of human personality. By depicting individuals as indifferent to others, it establishes a ephemeral lifestyle that stifles the ameliorating potential in them; "the limits of liberal democracy are the limits of self-preoccupied imagination."[35] In a liberal regime, individuals become exiles in their own society, only united in their separateness and self-interestedness. The dominant motif of liberal society is its tendency to anomie; individuals drift with no communal connections. Bereft of any sense of community, "our society may have become so anomic that explicit occasions for mutual recognition among strangers on public streets are more feared than sought."[36]

The difficulty with this individualistic ideology is that it ignores and suppresses actual human experience.[37] Individuals are located in history, within a context of allegiances. They are not abstract or bloodless, but are in part constituted by their social context. To divorce individuals from this structure of allegiances is to rob them of the "railings to which [individuals] can cling as they walk into the mist of their social lives."[38] It stunts the possibility of developing a set of shared ends and values, a precondition to the emergence of a genuine populist democratic practice. By developing a moral sense and practical experience of community, individuals will be better able to contribute to the growth of a shared set of values and institutions in accordance with which social life could be organized. Persons might come to be respected as themselves and not as simply rightholders. In this way, society could develop a modus vivendi that encourages caring and sharing and actualizes the possibility for meaningful connection with others.

(c) Adjudication and Social Change

Notwithstanding the corrosive implications of rights-based theories for communal aspirations, the Rule of Law might still be characterized as the ally of democracy. Democratic politics is usually thought to in-

---

35 Barber, *supra*, note 28 at p. 18.

36 R. Burt, *Taking Care of Strangers* (1979), p. 41.

37 For a development of this argument, see A. Hutchinson and P. Monahan, "The 'Rights' Stuff: Roberto Unger and Beyond" (1984), 62 Texas Law Review 1477 at 1534–37.

38 R. Dahrendorf, *Life Chances: Approaches to Social and Political Theory* (1979), p. 32.

volve a utilitarian calculus of the general welfare. There is no guarantee that this calculus will be conducted in a principled manner. Individual claims to autonomy and personhood might be ignored or bypassed simply in order to further the ephemeral interests of the community as a whole. On this view, the Rule of Law is required in order to ensure that considerations of principle and individual right enter into the societal calculus. The institution of judicial review is an attempt to transform a jungle of deals into a world of rights. As Ronald Dworkin urges, judicial review promises that "the deepest, most fundamental conflicts between individual and society will once, someplace, finally, become questions of justice."[39]

A sensitivity for individual rights might be seen as particularly apposite and necessary in contemporary society. Individual life is dominated and permeated by large and complex bureaucracies, principally the state and the business corporation. The challenge to individual rights is no longer the lynch mob crying for blood, but the coolly rational bureaucrat, armed with spread sheets and cost-benefit studies. Regard for the Rule of Law is thought to ensure that "social managers" will not trample individuals in the march toward so-called organizational progress. Yet, while bureaucracy represents one of the greatest threats to genuine democratic values, there is little reason to suppose that the Rule of Law offers any refuge from the dangers of unbridled bureaucracy.

The Rule of Law is premised on a set of beliefs about the relation between adjudication and social behaviour. It assumes that judicial decisions are a significant and positive instrument for shaping popular attitudes and social action. As an explanation of social change, the account is simplistic and lacks any empirical foundation. Indeed, the gathering of social data to ground their instrumental assumptions forms no part of the agenda of traditional jurisprudence. The limited available evidence suggests that the public is only vaguely aware of judicial activity and that there is little correlation between judicial pronouncements and societal life. For instance, numerous opinion surveys confirm that the public has only marginal awareness of legal institutions and decisions. Only half of Americans can recall any Supreme Court decision. Those who can have an unfavourable opinion of it, by a margin of at least two to one. Further, Americans have less public confidence in the Supreme Court than the Presidency or Congress.[40]

---

39 Dworkin, *supra*, note 22 at p. 71.
40 See Adamany and Grossman, "Support for the Supreme Court as a National Policymaker" (1983), 5 Law and Policy Quarterly 405.

It is instructive to track the direction of public opinion over time towards visible court decisions that are thought to be liberally enlightened. In the 1960s, both the school desegregation and reapportionment decisions of the American Supreme Court were favoured by about 60 per cent of respondents, while the school prayer decisions were opposed by a margin of about three to one.[41] By the 1970s, large majorities remained opposed to the school prayer decisions. In contrast, the reapportionment decisions were no longer visible to the public, while public support for the Court's desegregation decisions had eroded drastically. Although a majority of respondents remained committed to desegregation in schools, the judicial remedy of busing was opposed by 82 per cent of whites and 33 per cent of blacks.

Not surprisingly, in view of this ignorance or hostility towards adjudication, judicial decisions have not tended to bring about large-scale social change. For instance, although only about school desegregation, *Brown* is heralded by received jurisprudential wisdom as a turning point in relations between American blacks and whites and as a victory over Southern institutional racism. Yet, for almost a decade after *Brown*, the local situation of blacks remained appalling: "the Southern caste system remained intact . . . [and] the federal government's efforts on behalf of oppressed blacks were sporadic and ineffective."[42] It was not until the blacks mobilized themselves en masse in the early 1960s that their situation improved. The contribution that the *Brown* decision made to this state of affairs is moot and certainly not explained by the causally reductive accounts of Rule of Law theorists.

While racist attitudes and overt institutional practices may have improved, systemic racism persists. Some hard facts make for distressing reading. The poverty rate for black Americans is three times that of whites; non-white American men earn about 80 per cent of the wages of their white counterparts; the income gap between white and black families has widened since 1977; not only is the unemployment rate among blacks more than double that for whites, this unemployment inequality has itself doubled in the last thirty years; and while 26 per cent of young black high school graduates are unemployed, the exact same proportion of young white high school dropouts are unemployed.[43] Even

---

41 The survey data is collected and analysed in Adamany and Grossman, *ibid.* at 422–424.

42 S. Bachmann, "Lawyers, Law, and Social Change" (1985), 13 N.Y. Rev. of Law & Soc. Change 1.

43 See Cohen and Rogers, *supra*, note 1 at 30–32.

in the limited area of school desegregation itself, the immediate and long-term effects of *Brown* are moot. Like Dicken's Jarndyce v. Jarndyce, the *Brown* saga "drones on" and "still drags its dreary length before the Court."[44] The gap between legal doctrine and social change is striking. The rosy picture of social life painted by the legal materials is far removed from its sombre actuality.

(d) Of Vitamins and Virtues

The reasons for discussing the impact of court decisions is not to suggest that the American Supreme Court's civil rights or school prayer decisions were somehow "wrong". Such a conclusion would be beside the point. The meaningful issue is why an elite judiciary should have responsibility for making such decisions in the first place. Reliance on the Supreme Court undermines popular control and participation in the policy-making process. Although the Supreme Court receives extensive attention in the media and the law reviews, publicity is no substitute for participation and does not overcome the exclusion of citizens from such debate. The media is dominated by much the same elite voices and institutional actors as litigation. For citizens, Supreme Court judges seem to resemble inscrutable Platonic figures who make decisions in which they have no part and of which they are largely ignorant. When a decision does come to their attention, they are likely to disagree with it. This further decreases the extent to which individuals have control over their own lives.

The citizens' role as distant spectators is exacerbated by the arcane and stylized language of constitutional litigation. As disputes move into the magnetic field of law, they are translated into the received argot. To partake of the law's special privileges and prizes, citizens must become proficient in its idioms and nuances. In this way, legal discourse enforces its own canons of relevance, rationality and reasonableness. The lawyerly sentinels of power ensure that citizens comport to the rules of constitutional grammar; those who do not are deprived of a voice and are rendered powerless. The courts' historical function has not been to express popular justice, but rather "to ensnare it, control it and to strangle

---

44 See *Bleak House* (1853), ch. 1. See *Brown v. Bd. of Ed.*, 84 F.R.D. 383 (D. Kan. 1979) (seeking intervention in original Topeka desegregation case on behalf of class represented by Linda Brown's daughter); *Clark v. Bd. of Ed.*, 705 F. 2d 265 (8th Cir. 1983) (continuation of Little Rock desegregation case).

it, by re-inscribing it within institutions which are typical of a state apparatus."[45]

Defenders of this "elitist" approach to the Rule of Law must inevitably rely on some version of the claim that the ends justify the means. Although the elimination of popular control might be lamentable in the abstract, in cases like *Brown* it was the only realistic means available to counter deep-rooted and widespread public prejudice. Popular control, it is argued, would have been a recipe for the continued denial of justice and equality towards blacks. As such, it was simply unacceptable.

There is a good deal of force in these arguments. Given the harsh and brutal history of discrimination in the American South, it is difficult not to welcome the intervention of the Supreme Court as an antidote to racial intolerance. The difficulty with framing the debate in these terms is that it portrays the courts as an enlightened oracle proclaiming the gospel to the stupefied masses. Such an assumption is unwarranted and ahistorical; advances in social justice have been achieved through legislative rather than judicial action. Both Canadian and American courts have been as much a source of reaction and chauvinism as of edification and enlightenment. Much of the social welfare legislation enacted by the federal government in the 1930s was ruled unconstitutional by the courts as an intrusion on provincial jurisdiction. The practical effect of these decisions, such as the *Unemployment Insurance Reference* of 1937, was to make the enactment of such legislation impossible since the provinces lacked the fiscal resources to undertake such costly programs. The judicial decision in this particular instance was overcome only after the political branches of government secured a constitutional amendment which specifically empowered the federal government to put in place an unemployment insurance scheme.

The evolution of American First Amendment doctrine provides further illustration of this. Prior to World War I, the Court ruled in favour of a free speech claimant on only one occasion.[46] In subsequent decades the Court became more sensitive to free speech issues, but it cut back or ignored these doctrines during the so-called "Red Scare" in the 1950s. The 1960s was a period of renewed first amendment activism by the Court, coincident with the civil rights movement. However, in recent

---

45 M. Foucault, *Power/Knowledge: Selected Interviews and Other Writings*, ed. C. Gordon (1980), p. 1.

46 *American School of Magnetic Healing v. McAnnulty*, 187 U.S. 94 (1902). For a discussion, see Rabban, "The First Amendment in Its Forgotten Years" (1981), 90 Yale Law Journal 514.

years the first amendment has been enlisted as a potent weapon in the defence of the entrenched status of power and privilege. The ability of corporations and the wealthy to dominate the political process has been constitutionally guaranteed;[47] privately-owned public areas have been excluded from first amendment scrutiny;[48] while commercial advertising has been protected.[49] In short, while popular decision-making does not guarantee enlightened answers to political questions, neither does deference to an elite judiciary.

Even in the so-called "progressive" constitutional decisions, the difficult question is whether the elimination of popular control in favour of an elite institution like the Supreme Court will actually promote the long-term cause of justice and equality. At the institutional level, there may be a marked negative effect. Because judicial decisions tend to persuade people that things are being done, reformative energy may be frustrated and other governmental institutions may feel relieved of the pressure and responsibility to initiate and facilitate social change. Moreover, the assumption seems to be that values such as justice and freedom can be defined in some external forum, like the Supreme Court, and then simply foisted on a recalcitrant public. But the reality is precisely the opposite. Public values cannot be abstractly manufactured in some antiseptic political laboratory and administered, like vitamin tablets, to a malnourished and lethargic mass.

Values such as justice and equality are the products of politics, not its antecedents. They take root in a public that engages in debate and argument and that is given the opportunity to nurture notions of reasonableness and commonality. Deprived of such empowerment, public values corrode and civic energy dissipates. Deferring to "specialists", citizens lose the capacity to define their own values and traditions. Public morality will atrophy rather than be energized. The appointment of the judicial philosopher king exacerbates the problem it was intended to remedy.

Democracy means the greatest possible engagement by people in the greatest possible range of communal tasks and public action. As people reclaim control over their own lives, they will develop an appetite and a talent for more. This rejects the prevailing pessimism about the competence of ordinary citizens; their present apathy and disaffection is a product of their current powerlessness rather than any natural infirmity.

---

47 *Buckley v. Valeo*, 424 U.S. 1 (1976).
48 *Hudgens v. NLRB*, 424 U.S. 507 (1976).
49 *Virginia Pharmacy Board v. Virginia Consumer Council*, 425 U.S. 748 (1976).

This insight is easily forgotten in a setting in which the opportunities for meaningful popular participation are few. The central importance of participation and debate in the shaping of public morality can only be grasped by focussing on an institution which rejects values of expertise and elitism in favour of participatory self-government.

Such an institution is the jury system. To suggest that the jury system represents a paradigm of democratic practice may seem anachronistic or naïve. Critics on both the right and the left have condemned the jury as a device to legitimate bigotry, ignorance or racism. These criticisms of the jury parallel those issued against democracy in general; the basic complaints are that these institutions produce decisions that are oppressive and that individual citizens are incapable of making such decisions.

Yet, whatever the failings of individual juries, the jury system as a whole embodies to a remarkable degree values of self-government.[50] The jury system rejects rule by experts; people assume the responsibility for making important civic decisions on a rotating basis. Discussion and argument are central to the success of the institution. The jurors do not simply observe the trial and then cast their votes individually in the privacy of a polling booth. They are expected to arrive at a common verdict, through persuasion and argument. Without such debate, "the jury system as a whole would be devalued, and . . . individual jurors would value their own roles less."[51] The jury system represents a commitment to the principle that the ordinary citizen is competent to debate and decide important issues in the community. As E.P. Thompson states,[52]

> I can imagine better laws and I can imagine better jurors, but I cannot imagine a better system. I would like to think of the jury system as a lingering paradigm of an alternative mode of participatory self-government, a nucleus around which analogous modes might grow in our town halls, factories and streets.

With its emphasis on persuasion, argument and consensus, it is democratic rule writ small. True, the jury often acts as a rubber stamp for state values, but it can also act as a lamp of liberty which might illuminate the potential and power of ordinary people.

There is no quick fix for bigotry or prejudice. Certainly, it would be naïve to suppose that such deplorable attitudes would simply disap-

---

50 For discussion, see E.P. Thompson, *Writing by Candlelight* (1980), pp. 167–170; M. Walzer, *Spheres of Justice: A Defense of Pluralism and Equality* (1983), pp. 308–309.

51 Walzer, *ibid.*, at 309.

52 Thompson, *supra*, note 50 at 170.

pear with the dawn of a genuine democratic community. Democracy does not guarantee civic enlightenment. But if communal morality is to become more informed and developed, this will be achieved through more rather than less democracy. It is only through public talk that small minded or superficial attitudes might be exposed and attacked. The ambition is not to attain some romantic or utopian harmony, but a political order which facilitates individual participation in the continuing social deliberation over political ends.

Judicial musing, enforced by fiat, is no substitute for civic deliberation. Rule by judiciary supposes that the only way to deter oppression is to impose external restraints on the political process. But because such restraints deny the moral competence of citizens, they undermine the very process of reflection and self-criticism which might lead to a more mature collective morality. Elitist politics breed only a mob; the nurturing of citizens demands democratic culture.

3. CONSTRUCTION AND CONSTRAINT

The Rule of Law democrat lives in a society bereft of community. Given its historical obsession with abstract individual rights and liberties, liberal legalism stymies the establishment of a truly communal modus vivendi in which people can satisfy their collective and personal aspirations. Within a legalistic ethic, communal ambitions are destined to remain etiolated. We have tried to free democracy from its bondage to the Rule of Law. Emancipated, it might serve rather than stifle the flourishing of communal life and fulfilled citizens.

A concrete and constructive example illustrates our claims. The way modern society defines "health" and "need" and establishes standards for health care both exposes the elitism of present arrangements and suggests the possibilities for democratic involvement. Currently, the medical and legal professions have come together in an unholy alliance to monopolize the process of health decision-making. People have become "limp and mystified voyeur[s]"[53] on the treatment of their own bodies, the passive objects of clinical therapy rather than active participants in its prescription and administration. In contrast to present practice, democracy demands that people must be fully integrated into the formulation of any preventative and rehabilitative program. All individuals must become "welfare workers"; "a society which ignores [that health care involves mutual learning, mutual help and mutual responsibility]

---

53 I. Illich, *Limits to Medicine*, ch. 3 (1976).

may stave off, for a time, the effects of illness and injury, only to pave a better road to ill-health."[54]

Even the fully democratic society will have to make "tragic choices" about the allocation of scarce resources. While medical technology advances apace, its direction and nature are not open to public control. Much medical research has been devoted to the reduction of mortality, but this has meant a corresponding increase in morbidity, especially among the elderly. Choices about the treatment of defective babies, geriatrics, paraplegics and other afflicted individuals have been made in the elite forums of the medical and legal establishment; they deserve to be the subject of a more thoroughgoing democratic debate. The target must be the introduction of communal health care services which work toward a local and supportive environment for recovery or readjustment to changed health circumstances.

There must develop a greater appreciation that health and welfare are as much socially caused as individually experienced. This means the fostering of a more holistic approach to well-being. This would not merely treat individual symptoms, but would concern itself with the total environment in which people live, work, play and die. The control of risk would be of, at least, the same importance as the treatment of injury and misfortune. Whereas the democratic society takes an integrated and coherent stance on risk and well-being, the liberal society adopts a divided and contradictory position.[55]

A commitment to democracy does not mean that constraints on popular decision making must always and everywhere be condemned. It is important that the basic institutions and practices of democracy— free elections, debate and assembly—be guaranteed and extended. Further, democracy implies the necessity for general laws which do not single out particular groups or individuals for special treatment and which are applied in nondiscriminatory fashion across the whole community. But there is a distinction between constitutional safeguards which constrain democratic activity in the name of democracy and those which constrain democratic activity in the name of "right answers". The latter type of constraints seek to substitute the judgments of philosophy for those of the people simply because the popular judgments are regarded as tainted. As Michael Walzer observes,[56]

---

54 A.V. Campbell, *Medicine, Health and Justice: The Problem of Priorities* (1978), p. 88.
55 These ideas are developed further in A. Hutchinson, "Beyond No-Fault" (1985), 60 Cal. L. Rev. 755. See also, R. Abel, "A Socialist Approach to Risk" (1982), 41 Maryland L. Rev. 695.
56 M. Walzer, "Philosophy and Democracy" (1981), 9 Political Theory 379 at 392–93.

. . . any extensive incorporation of philosophical principles into the law . . . is . . . to take them out of the political arena where they properly belong. The interventions of philosophers should be limited to the gifts they bring. Else they are like Greeks bringing gifts, of whom the people' should beware, for what they have in mind is the capture of the city.

Democrats should always be wary of constraints that seek to substitute the cold hand of philosophy for popular judgment, no matter how presently plausible or attractive they might appear. Of course, instances will arise in which public sentiments appear so wrong-headed that they demand instant repudiation. Even a committed democrat would likely be tempted by the siren song of the Rule of Law. But to tie oneself to the post of "principle" is to court seduction rather than salvation. Far from purifying public morality, it would merely ensure its continued debasement.

The Rule Of Law:
Is That The Rule That Was?

Philippe Nonet

Before I come to my topic, I must first ask you to grant me a small request, which is to suspend our understanding that this talk is part of a lecture series. I want your permission to address you not as an instructor would lecture his pupils, but instead as a teacher—particularly a law teacher—might confide in his colleagues. I am sure you will find it quite easy to grant me that favour. All of you have at times been called upon to teach others, and have therefore learned how to assume the role of teacher. In addition, as Emile Durkheim points out, since all teachers, whatever their specialties, teach first and foremost "the impersonal authority of the rule,"[1] all teachers are law teachers. Therefore, the role of law teacher holds no mystery to you. At the same time, it is rather important to me that you agree to take the part. I am obligated to speak to you, as I promised long ago, but I fear that what I have to say may not be the sort of things a teacher would properly tell his students. As you know, some thoughts, however true, are at certain times and in certain contexts much better left unsaid. Perhaps the thoughts that follow are unsuitable to a lecture, but I should think it perfectly proper to share them in confidence with fellow teachers. Thus by assuming that role, a gesture you can perform with great ease, you can free me from a difficult ethical dilemma, and save me the painful agony of choosing, and then doing, the lesser wrong. Thank you.

The problem upon which I should like to reflect with you concerns the responsibilities we have for the moral education of our students. That

---

1 Emile Durkheim, *Moral Education* (translation by E.K. Wilson and H. Schnurer, New York: The Free Press, 1961), p. 156.

is the reason why it is best discussed first among us, in relative privacy, while our pupils are out of the room. Imagine I have just finished delivering my annual series of lectures on the Rule of Law. Several students raise their hands and ask: "Is that still the rule in this land?" What should I answer? In asking you this question, I may well seem to have made the students' question my own, and then to have addressed it to you. But such is not my intention at all. I know what a truthful answer to their question would be. My question is whether that is the answer I should give them. Of course I owe them the truth, but I owe them other obligations as well. As you know, some truths must at times and in certain contexts remain unsaid.

Suppose the anthropological evidence warranted grave doubts as to the "existence" of the Rule of Law in our land. If I were an anthropologist reporting to my fellow anthropologists about my studies of this tribe, I should have to say that the Rule of Law seemed to have only the weakest hold upon the tribe. However, the question did not arise at a professional meeting of anthropologists. It arose in a classroom, where I was asked to speak as a teacher, that is, as an officer of the tribe, responsible for professing its laws. If in that capacity I stated the anthropological truth, which I know, would I not be professing lawlessness? Isn't it true that such a profession would violate the duty I owe to the moral education of my students? Of course I can evade this duty by resigning the office, and perhaps also relinquishing my citizenship, but only extraordinary circumstances would justify such a flight from one's station. Must I then speak falsely?

1. RECHTSSTAAT (LE DROIT)

Some of us will argue that my chief duty is to the truth; in fact, I suspect all of us think so some of the time. We are all realists, at times. We are all at times inclined to accord primacy to truth. *Fiat veritas, pereat mundus*, proclaims the modern mind. No one here is impervious to that call. Who here has not at times read, thought, spoken, or indeed written, of "the death of law", or of "the end of liberalism", or of the "crisis" that law and liberty have undergone, or of the "decline" or "twilight" that now awaits these noble and old institutions?[2] Few of us moderns will steadily succeed at contradicting the child in ourselves, when he finds that the Emperor wears no clothes. I shall argue against the child—

---

2 For an example, see Theodore Lowi, *The End of Liberalism* (New York: W.W. Norton, 1969).

the modern, the realist—in ourselves. But before I do so, I must acknowledge how hard it is to resist him, and how much patience and forgiveness we owe ourselves when we yield. In fact, it is almost impossible nowadays to explain what the Rule of Law is (or would be, if it were) without causing oneself, and any reasonably alert observer of our world, to doubt that it still exists. Hence, my students' doubts. I can still hear the irony of their question.

(In parenthesis, I should mention the possibility that they did not doubt enough. Their question, "Is that still the rule in this land?" seems to assume that the Rule *was*, though perhaps it no longer is. Recall that I was lecturing in California, part of a land about which one may well doubt that it ever formed a state;[3] if it never formed a state, it never was a *Rechtsstaat*, a state under the Rule of Law. Hegel, among others, thought the United Colonies, not States, of America were the land of the future, that is, a dreamland where, like the White Queen's jam,[4] the Rule of Law forever *would* be.[5] As our song says, "We shall overcome." Freedom tomorrow, no freedom today. Of course Hegel may have been mistaken; we have it on the authority of John Adams that the Commonwealth of Massachusetts, for one, constituted itself as "a government of laws, not men."[6] Be that as it may. My point is only that the past and future existence of the Rule of Law are just as questionable as the present. With respect to the past and future, however, I see less objection to letting the truth prevail. Let the realists and other fortune tellers occupy these domains. My worries are with doubts concerning the present, for it is presently that we act, presently that we may or may not have obligations respecting our actions, presently that laws may or may not govern us, presently that the "existence" of laws may matter as a practical question. Now that question cannot be left for the realist to answer.)

What had I said, to cause my students such doubts? I had definitely not said that the Rule of Law does not exist among us. These were highly attentive students; they would not have asked the question if I had al-

3 Hegel, *Philosophy of History* (translation by J. Sibree, New York: Dover Publications, 1956), pp. 84–87.

4 Lewis Carroll, *Through the Looking Glass*, in *The Annotated Alice* (New York: Clarkson N. Potter, 1960), p. 247.

5 Although Hegel did use the phrase "Land of the Future" to characterize the United Colonies, one may well wonder whether he shared this interpretation of its meaning. Hegel, *supra*, note 3, pp. 86–87.

6 John Adams, *The Report of a Constitution, or Form of Government, for the Commonwealth of Massachusetts*, 1779, in Charles Francis Adams, *The Works of John Adams* (Boston: Little, Brown, and Co., 1865), vol. IV, p. 230.

ready answered it in my lectures. Nor had I said the Rule does exist. I had only attempted to answer the question: what is this Rule of Law that sets people free? what is this liberty people gain from being so ruled? The texts upon which I had relied were mostly, but not only, translations from ancient Greek and old-fashioned German, chosen with no intention to suggest that the Rule is either foreign to us or a thing of the past, but only because the best explanations of the Rule happen to have been written long ago and in these foreign languages. My own words, not to mention my accent, also must have sounded alien and antiquarian. Listen to this (please allow me to quote from my notes): "A people is ruled by Law when its members live in a state of rectitude (*Rechtsstaat*)." "Freedom comes with personality, that is, the spiritual harmony of each member within himself, and of all members with each other." "The act by which we liberate ourselves is the act of atonement; the act by which we enslave ourselves is the act of estrangement." "Law is the Second Nature each person creates as he learns the language and customs of a moral community." Half the classroom was sighing, the other half chuckling; I can still hear them. I was not trying to be obscure; my job is to enlighten. I was only trying to teach my class the language with which one can speak of freedom under the Rule of Law.

I had begun the lectures with words that should have been intelligible to modern English speaking undergraduates. The words were borrowed from H.L.A. Hart, to whom English jurisprudence owes its present chance to recover consciousness of the grounds upon which law is built, that is, of its foundation in philosophy (*die Philosophie*). Here is the chance:

> [W]hen a social group has certain roles of conduct, . . . it is possible to be concerned with the rules, either merely as an observer who does not himself accept them, or as a member of the group which accepts and uses them as guides to conduct. We may call these respectively the 'external' and the 'internal points of view.'[7]

To be strictly correct, he should have said "standpoints" instead of "points of view," for it is only from the external standpoint that one has

---

7 H.L.A. Hart, *The Concept of Law* (Oxford: Clarendon Press, 1961), p. 86. The distinction leaves open the possibiity that the observer's own detached understanding of rules must be grounded in a prior understanding attained in the intimacy of membership.

a view, that is, that one observes.[8] From these words, it takes but a few steps to deduce the relevant parts of philosophy, all the way to and including Nietzsche and Freud. There indeed lies the germ of one of the most fertile thoughts in the history of spirit: namely, the distinction between man's rules as observer and as actor, or between theoretical (or reflective) and practical (or active) reason. As an observer, I ask myself: "What do I see?," and my question is answered by a description of the natural objects to which my eyes are directed. As an actor, I ask myself: "What will I do (say, think)?," and my question is answered by a decision, "I will," that legislates the universally right way to act under the circumstances. And my first prescription is to assume full membership in my people,[9] that I may learn and follow a way of life worth living.

Suppose I step out of the role of actor, and member of that community, and instead look at my actions from the standpoint of observer. I shall then think of myself and my social world objectively, in the third person and the neuter gender, as I should think of natural phenomena. Of him who takes that viewpoint, it may be said that (turning Freud on his head) "where *ego* was, there will be *id*." The actor, *ego*, who chooses what he shall do is replaced by an organism, *id*, powered by wants and beliefs, subject to the contingencies of its environment. The psychologist unseats the legislator. As we all know, this *id* is composed of two parts: one part is experienced as desire, and therefore easily recognized as instinctual *id*; the other, a disguised *id*, is experienced as *superego*, the conscience that frustrates desire and voices the demands of social control. And here we have the foundations of the metaphysics of modern ways, whereby individual—a specimen of the genus *homo sapiens*, unique because it has ben shaped by a unique combination of natural causes—struggles with society's demands for conformity, and forms the fantastic idea of a state of natural freedom, where he could gratify his wants without clashing with the contrary wants of society.

After a moment of reflection, the careful observer finds that what looked at first like a conflict between its wants and others' demands,

---

8 Kant had it right. See Kant, *Groundwork of the Metaphysic of Morals* (translation by H.J. Paton, New York: Harper Torchbooks, 1984), p. 118; p. 450 of the Royal Prussian Academy edition. Needless to say, a kind of "view" is also open from the third standpoint, that of the spectator, insofar as contemplation is the mode of his involvement in the world. See Kant's *Critique of Judgment*, which points to issues well beyond our present concerns. But see also *infra*, note 38 and the text it accompanies.

9 "What from your fathers you received as heir / Acquire, if you would possess it." Goethe, *Faust* (translation by W. Kaufman), line 682 f. See also Diogenes Laertius, VIII, 16.

rather consists of a conflict between two aspects of its own wants. The power that society has to frustrate my desires lies at bottom in my own desire to be approved, or loved, or not to be caused pain by others, or by their handmaiden, my conscience. The struggle between individual and society is a clash of two sides of my nature: one aspect of my wants causes me to long for independence and separateness from others, while another aspect of the same wants causes me to long for union with and dependence upon others. One side's fantasy is the other's nightmare. The freedom of which the individual dreams would promise either a state of war, in which all people must at all times be ready to "interfere with the liberty of action of any of their number for self-protection,"[10] or a state of radical isolation, in which each man's "independence is absolute,"[11] so that his actions "merely concern himself,"[12] and others are equally indifferent to "his own good, either physical or moral."[13] After contemplating this prospect in its starkness, I should want to "escape from freedom"[14] into submission. But the state envisioned in the opposite dream of a blissful union, where I should lose my separateness and gain love by serving others' wants, would make me want to escape from bondage. In fact, my organism, *id*, does not want either liberation from or submission to society; it is forever torn by its desires for both. It may therefore want for *superego* to achieve partial subjugation of *id*; and for *id* to enjoy occasional moments of indulgence with impunity. Perhaps at times it can gain the subservience of others to its wants; more likely it can find ways of hiding from the eyes of others to indulge its passions at lesser risk. It can indeed use for this purpose the walls of "privacy" that law protects (for reasons that must be entirely foreign to *id*'s desire for concealment).

As an observer, I cannot tell whether *id* is right in either wanting or not wanting either natural freedom, or submission, or hiding places where to enjoy forbidden fruits. From this standpoint, the laws that "govern the dealings of society with the individual in the ways of compulsion and control, whether the means used be physical force or the coercion of opinion,"[15] are just natural laws that lie in the province of

---

10 J.S. Mill, *On Liberty*, in *Collected Works*, vol. XVIII (Toronto: University of Toronto Press, 1977), p. 223.

11 *Ibid.*, p. 224.

12 *Ibid.*, p. 224.

13 *Ibid.*, p. 223.

14 Erich Fromm, *Escape From Freedom* (New York: Avon Books, 1941).

15 J.S. Mill, *supra*, note 10, p. 223.

the theoretical sciences of biology, psychology, or sociology. They cannot tell me what to prescribe for myself as an actor. *Id* does not act. *Id* is pure passion, acted upon by forces alien to itself.

To determine what I will do, I must switch out of the role of observer, and reassert myself as the author of my actions, having authority over my conduct. "Where *id* was, there shall *ego* be."[16] In these or other words or indeed no words at all, I establish myself as a spiritual being, an actor who chooses what by reason he requires, that is, the universally right way to act. *Ego* "obeys no law except that which he sets for himself,"[17] and he denies that "power can be exercised over him against his will,"[18] either by others (society) or by *id*'s (individual's) own natural inclinations. Free from the fantasy of natural freedom, also known as the despotism of the pleasure principle,[19] *ego* governs himself autonomously. This is the freedom that goes hand in hand with the Rule of Law, otherwise known as reason (*Vernunft*).

In that state, the *Rechtsstaat* or *Vernunftstaat*, there is no individual either at war with or subservient to society. Entities like individual and society exist only in the objective world of the theoretical mind. From the practical standpoint, there are only persons living in harmony within a spiritual community. Indeed it is questionable whether one may speak of "persons" in the plural; the mode of being of spiritual beings is to form a unity.[20] Look. Suppose you see me about to take the wrong step, and you stop and show me the right way, I will be grateful to you; I will correct myself, not because you (others, or society) prevailed upon me, but simply because I will. At law, no one wins or loses; only justice prevails. Furthermore, what is right in my case is universally right; it is part of a public knowledge we all share, and of a common good we all treasure. Thus the autonomous *Ego* is at one (atoned) with himself as well as with others, whom he also respects as persons. In other words *Ego* is the seat of personality; in action, the question "How can I

---

16 Freud, *New Introductory Lectures on Psychoanalysis* (translation by J. Strachey, New York: W.W. Norton, 1965), p. 80. Freud himself used the German not the Latin words. On the horrors done to Freud by the Latin and Greek of his English translation, see Bruno Bettelheim, *Freud and Man's Soul* (New York: A.A. Knopf, 1982).

17 Kant, *Groundwork of the Metaphysic of Morals*, p. 102; p. 434 of the Royal Academy edition.

18 J.S. Mill, *supra*, note 10, p. 223.

19 Freud, *Beyond the Pleasure Principle* (translation by J. Strachey, New York: Bantam Books, 1959).

20 Hegel, *Philosophy of Right* (translation by T.M. Knox, Oxford: Oxford University Press, 1952), paragraph 49, p. 44.

spiritualize desire?"[21] is answered, my and their desires are transformed into a harmony of ends, and our relations change into a union, such that we constitute a kingdom of ends.[22]

So I explained, and I stopped just at the point where jurisprudence begins to end in the beginning of theology. Then I found some of my best students were in a state of doubt. Witness the question they put to me. I knew the point at which I had begun to lose them. I had professed that there were no adversaries, hence no winners or losers, at the Bar of Justice. Unfortunately, they had heard before that trials at law are proceedings between adversaries in which each party's lawyer speaks for his client's interests! (By the way, it is not my intention here to accuse my colleagues in procedure and professional ethics of having taught heresy. For all I know, my students had learned these falsehoods long before they came to law school. Some heresies work like pollutants in the atmosphere: we breathe them from the day we are born, and we hardly notice as they slowly invade and soil our brains. In any event, it does not matter what caused my students to think as they did; it matters only that they thought as they did, and did not yet see their mistake.)

2. GESETZESSTAAT. (LA LOI)

And why did they not see it? Because it stemmed from another and deeper mistake, or rather a more elusive and more fatal instance of the same mistake, to which I had perhaps not yet given enough attention in my lectures. Briefly, they thought one does not know, or indeed think, what one cannot say. Hence, they concluded, the only rules of law we have (the rule of which would constitute the Rule of Law) are the rules (including principles, and theories explaining rules and principles) we have stated, and which thereby "pre-exist" action in such a way that action can be patterned after them. To my students, the Rule of Law could not be a state of rectitude (*Rechtsstaat*); it could only consist in a state of conformity to statements of law (*Gesetzesstaat*). Now there can be no harmony, or freedom, or indeed anything of spiritual worth in such a state. Indeed there is reason to doubt that it can exist.

Consider this problem. To know whether a particular case falls under a certain statement of law, we must (among other conditions)

---

21 Nietzsche, *Twilight of the Idols* (translation by R.J. Hollingdale, Penguin Books, 1968), p. 42.
22 Kant, *supra*, note 17, p. 100; p. 433 of the Royal Academy edition.

know what the statement means. Other rules, rules of language (semantics, grammar), must then tell us what the statement means. To be known, these rules also must be stated, and these statements must themselves derive their meaning from other rules that must be stated. And so on, *ad infinitum*. If this thesis were true, we could not speak; therefore we could not state, or know, or indeed think it. (In fact, surprisingly many people are able to say, think, and even think they know that "it is impossible to speak"; all realists are among them.[23] Nevertheless, by its own rules, the state of conformity to statements of law cannot exist.)

Perhaps one can solve this problem by allowing for rules of language an exception to the general rule that one does not know what one cannot state. (There is good ground for doing so; zillions of people have actually managed to become proficient at speaking without ever acquiring the ability to state the rules of grammar they followed. But is language exceptional in this respect?) However, this difficulty is only the first of a long series, the next of which arises from the truth that, even if their meaning can somehow be discerned, "general propositions do not decide concrete cases."[24] I do (*ego* does), and since all cases to be decided are concrete cases, all authority to decide is vested in my "discretion". The obvious, but not the main, reason for my having such discretion, is that statements of law are abstract, and can therefore at best tell us only what is right in general. Only if this case exhibited exactly and only the features that are abstracted in existing statements of law, would the right action be one that exhibited exactly and only the features abstracted in the statements. But my problem is not to find and do what is right in general, or in the abstracted world of statements of law, but to decide and do what is right in *this* case, that is, to do the concrete act that is universally (not generally) right under these unique and concrete circumstances (which may or may not fit the abstract model). All this is just another way of saying with the Philosopher that "in the matter of practical affairs, it is not possible to make general statements that are correct; hence the equitable is the just, a rectification of laws that fall short by virtue of their generality."[25] All statements of law must be qualified by a *ceteris paribus* clause. Or, to put it like the modern Socrates,

---

23 See, for example, Fred Rodell, *Woe Unto You Lawyers* (Berkeley Publishing Co. ed., 1980), pp. 107–122.

24 O.W. Holmes dissenting in *Lochner v. New York,* 198 U.S. 45, 76 (1905).

25 Aristotle, *Nicomachean Ethics*, Book V, Ch. X, 4–7. To hear it from his master's voice, read Plato, *Politics*, St. II, 294–297.

"the universal imperative is as follows: 'Act as though the maxim *of your action* [this present action of yours which will never be repeated] were by your will to become a universal law [to recur eternally].'"[26] These truths, and much more, I had explained to my students, and they had followed me, though not without some difficulty when we came to the idea of a concrete universal.

Having come this far, however, they found themselves in an impossible position: from the truth that "there are no rules for the application of rules,"[27] they concluded that we knew of no way to decide any case rightly. If the only rules we have are the rules we have stated, and statements of law do not decide any case, then: (i) the discretionary judgment by which a case is decided must be lawless caprice; and (ii) the rules we have stated are not knowledge of the right way to act. Perhaps I can (form the illusion that I) conform to them, or depart from them and do something else, but I cannot act either justly or unjustly, since I do not know what is right. Whatever I do, I do without reason. My real world is a state of nature, of *it*ness, of necessity instead of freedom: *I* (*ego*) do not decide or act; *it* (*id*) is caused to behave. It is at times caused to (appear to) conform to these statements of law, in part by others who are caused to cause it to (appear to) conform, and whom (which?) it is at times caused to (appear to) resist, in part by others (including lawyers) who are caused to cause it to (appear to) resist. So thought my students. No wonder they also thought that at law people are at war with one another. No wonder they thought that words at law were just weapons, means of obfuscating, confusing, and manipulating others.

I tried to rescue them. They were right, I said, in denying authority to statements of law, but they had not yet inquired deep enough into the reason for their conclusion. Statements of law have no authority, because they are not Law (*Recht*): they are only descriptions of law (*Gesetz*).[28] They are factual, not normative statements. They are products of the intellect, or the reflective mind (*Verstand*), that is, the mind examining its own spontaneous activity, and therefore thinking from the external

---

26 Kant, *supra*, note 17, p. 89; p. 421 of the Royal Academy edition. The explanations in brackets are inspired by Nietzsche, *The Gay Science* (translation by W. Kaufman, New York: Vintage Books, 1974), aphorism 341, pp. 273–274.

27 Kant, *Critique of Pure Reason*, first edition, pp. 131–134; second edition, pp. 170–173.

28 This is no place to essay a theory of legislation, but clearly the chief principle of such a theory is that statutes are declarative, not creative of law. On this, even Hegel agrees with Locke: "made" law is unjust. Hegel, *Philosophy of Right*, paragraph 212, p. 136.

standpoint.[29] Here we have the observer observing what the actor appears to think, that is, treating *ego* as *id*, as part of a nature that exists for the mind as an object of experience. He can do so because what I think as I act is the second nature I have formed, as indeed I must, in order to live a good life; it consists of the dispositions of mind and body (the skills, habits, virtues, learned by repeated exercise) that enable me spontaneously to recognize the right way to act, and to perform accordingly, with ease, grace, and a kind of pleasure. Our second nature manifests itself in the regularities of life to which we attach the *opinio necessitatis*, and which are therefore called our customs (what is fitting and proper) or traditions (what we must teach our neophytes) or law (the right way to live).[30]

Of this second nature, as of the first, the intellect acquires knowledge in the form that distinguishes intellectual knowing, namely generalizations (statements of law) ordered systematically to compose theories. The word "theory", meaning what is visible to the reflective mind, is an obvious indication that theories of, say, justice, morality, settled law, etc., have no practical authority. Of this knowing, indeed it is true that if one cannot state it one does not have it. But what one misses then is just a factual report, that has validity only for the intellect in its activity as observer, in this case as self-consciousness applying itself to practical reason. To the actor, his second nature matters as what he is in himself (*an sich*), not as what it is for the intellect (*für sich*). In itself, this second nature also consists of knowledge, but of a kind quite different from intellectual knowing. This kind is practical knowledge of *how* acts are performed, not intellectual knowledge *that* they must be performed in such and such specified ways; it is learned through practice, by participation *in*, familiarity, intimacy *with*, its object (if one may still speak of "objects" of this mode of knowing), not by observation of it from without; in other words, it is an art, not a science, namely the art of living.

Then suddenly I felt as though I had run into a wall, a wall of skepticism. My students seemed determined not to follow this train of thoughts. "Anti-intellectual," I heard them mutter. Why? Perhaps, I thought, their objections were bound to the setting in which we were, and the roles we occupied in it. Remember. I was lecturing on the rule of law. Now a distinctive feature of lecturing is the effort to teach and

---

29 Hegel, *Philosophy of Right*, paragraph 211, p. 134.
30 *Ibid.*, paragraphs 4 and 151, pp. 20, 108.

learn law by stating it; hence, there, one uses theories of the law as doctrines, stated for perusal in schools, *ad docendum*. In that setting, both teacher and student are expected to stretch the powers of the intellect in order that it grasp as much of the law as it possibly can. This is why, by the way, intellectuals are generally preferred to serve in the role of lecturer, and why intellectually inclined students are generally more successful in lecture courses. Now I had just lectured about the limits of the powers of intellect, and the limits of what can be learned in lecture. I had said that law is an art learned by practice, by actually making oneself an incarnation of spirit. That is why, by the way, it is taught mainly in apprenticeship, not in lecture courses; it must be shown, it cannot truly be said. But there was nothing anti-intellectual in my remarks. They themselves were products of intellect; they invoked theoretical knowledge, that the intellect itself has of the nature and limits of its own powers; they were meant as just a friendly reminder.

The reminder was this: if the intellect is to exercise its theoretical powers (as indeed it should; practical reason invites us to the reflection), it must have objects upon which these powers actually can be exercised. Hence it must not allow itself to destroy the nature, in this case the Second Nature, the embodied spirit, it is given to observe. In order to flourish the intellect must acknowledge its own dependence upon a practical knowledge of which it can form at best an incomplete and tentative representation. Unfortunately, as we know, the intellect is at times affected by a self-destructive *hubris*. It is at times tempted to usurp the supreme authority of practical reason, that is to claim for its own assertions, statements of law, an authority that can only be vested in Law. Then, moved by its own laws (called logic, in the narrow sense), it discovers there is no way from *Gesetz* to *Recht*, from statements of law to right action, from a *Verstandesstaat* to the *Vernunftstaat*, and it draws the suicidal conclusion that there is no possible knowledge of a right way to act. Suicidal indeed because if there can be no law, there can be no reflection upon law; nothing can be said about law, nothing can be lectured about law, and law schools as we know them have nothing to teach. Some of my colleagues are known to deny there is law, even as they lecture on law, but it is rather obvious that they do not mean their speech as serious practical talk; after all, lecturing allows room for comedy.

Let us then, I said, save the intellect, if only for its own sake, for the sheer love of it, from its self-destructiveness. Let us recall it to its duty of deference to practical reason. Logic (in the narrow sense) may then rule in its proper domain, which is the intellectual ordering of descriptive statements of law; articulate consistency, sometimes called formal rationality *is* a quality of explanations of the law. But in action we seek rightness, not consistency, and there is no such thing as formal justice.[31] There, like Churchill, we let ourselves be guided not by logic, but by custom.[32] Of that we have intimate knowledge. And rhetorically I asked: how could any knowledge, particularly intellectual knowledge, be more perfect than knowledge by intimate acquaintance? Would the holy spirit consist of propositions? "In the beginning was the act," not the Word.[33] This, I think, is the point at which I finally lost the class. "Illiberal," I heard them mutter. Angrily several students invoked a statement of law which, they said, forbade appeals to the authority of God in a public classroom (remember I was lecturing as an Officer of Instruction of the State—or is it a Colony?—of California).[34] Yet earlier the same students had admitted that statements of law cannot point the right way.

3. MACHTSTAAT? (LA FORCE?)

In defence of my students, we should bear in mind certain circumstances that mitigated their mistake. First, they did not have the benefit of having been brought up in a language that made the distinction between acting and observing familiar to its speakers, and most knew only their native dialect. From early childhood, a native French speaker knows (is familiar with) how it is possible to *connaître* (*kennen*) without *savoir* (*wissen*); and he has no difficulty later in grasping intellectually that someone can *connaître son droit sans savoir ce que dit la loi*. So do German speakers. But English has only one word for each of these two pairs: know, and law. How confusing.

Second my students were young, and youth must rebel at the thought one must practice and age before one can lay claim to knowledge of law. In fact, in the Land of the Future, where perhaps we were, such a thought would have been almost unthinkable. In such a land, people would abhor their past and then forget it, despise and then abandon their elderly members, criticize and reject all things traditional as such. But youth as such, they would adore, because a new generation promises new ideas, and the new as such would be the sole object of their pursuits.

---

31 David Lyons, "Formal Justice," (1973), 58 Cornell Law Review 833.

32 Winston S. Churchill, *Closing the Ring* (Bantam Books, 1962), p. 146. See also Friedrich Nietzsche, *The Anti-Christ*, paragraph 14 (translation by R.J. Hollingdale, Penguin Books, 1968),p. 125: "We deny that anything can be made perfect so long as it is still made conscious."

33 Goethe, *Faust*, Part I, verse 1237: "Im Anfang war die Tat."

34 By contrast, the coat of arms that hung above the podium from which this lecture was read, bore the inscription: "Dieu et mon droit."

There the old would beg for attention by dressing like teenagers. And all would forever exhaust themselves in innovation, for the new can never be: the new cannot be found, since the old, by the measure of which the novelty of the new is determined, has been condemned to oblivion; furthermore as the new comes into being (unnoticed), it already has lost its novelty. Thus, the Land of the Future would endure the torture of Sisyphus, which is just the fate it would deserve for its foolish pursuit. Nothing is worthy of esteem in the young, or the new, or the future as such; they represent only innocence, that is, the purely abstract and unrealized possibility of right action; whereas only the actual is right, and worthy of esteem.[35]

Perhaps indeed we were in the Land of the Future. If so, my students (little did they know) were in fact right in denying we were subject to the Rule of Law. Ours was a government of men, not laws, a state of might (*Machtstaat*), not right, and the classroom in which we met was (little did I know) located in a School of Social Warfare.[36] No wonder my students thought themselves slaves, subject only and entirely to forces of natural necessity. Was this not in fact the land which had abolished the slavery of some by coercing all into equality, thereby making slavery universal? What then was I to say in answer to their question?

And at that moment, the answer I would give appeared under a light so shining that I could not refuse to see it. Clearly, my first duty was to freedom, particularly to my students' emancipation from the slavery in which they held themselves. They had to be shown how to walk through the walls of factuality—the state of nature—in which they had imprisoned themselves, into the free world of spirit. Therefore, my first step in carrying out my duty was to refuse hearing the question as they put it. For the question insidiously invited me also to take the standpoint from which it had been asked, that is, the standpoint of an observer looking at himself and others from without, like a stranger to, the spiritual realm, and hence from without and like a stranger to himself as a person in that realm. In accepting that invitation, I would have accepted, and thereby confirmed, the state of mutual estrangement (the learned say "alienation") in which they were holding us. I would have lent my assent

---

35 Hegel, *Philosophy of Right*, preface, p. 10. See also Aristotle, *Nicomachean Ethics*, Book I, Ch. III, 5–7.

36 Objection: if there was a school, there was a Law School. (See above footnote 1, and the text it accompanies.) If there was a Law School, there was Law, and so on. Then perhaps there was no school, no classroom, no teacher, and even I did not exist, Descartes to the contrary notwithstanding.

to my own and to their disenfranchisement, my own and their deper-
sonalization. What was called for instead was a denial of estrangement,
that is, an act of atonement (*Versöhnung*), of making oneself at one with
others, an affirmation of one's unity with others in spirit. Anything else
would have been sheer nihilism. How would I atone?

I toyed briefly with the idea of explaining away the *Machtstaat* they
saw by reinterpreting their evidence from the internal standpoint. I could
have shown them that the lawlessness they observed should rather be
judged unlawful conduct; to notice a breach of the law is to affirm the
law's authority, but to deny the existence of the Rule of Law is to agree
that no unlawful act can be committed, and hence that we are all pure
innocent youth. I could have shown them further that many acts that
would seem either lawless or unlawful under their description were mis-
characterized by that description. For example, when friends think of
each other, their minds are said to be filled with thoughts of each other's
desires, pleasures and pains, victories and defeats; this description makes
them seem either lawless or corrupt until at last one notes that they are
friends; they are thinking benevolently, which is just what friends must.
Similarly, lawyers and judges are said to argue or decide cases by "applying" statements of law to the facts of the cases; this description makes
them seem either lawless or unjust; in fact, however, they are just fulfil-
ling a most important duty, namely that of civil respect, or the duty to
accord each other what Hannah Arendt called "the relevance of speech,"
and thus to assert our commitment to the spiritual unity we form. The
intellect does wonders in helping us discharge this duty, though only if
it knows its limits and accepts the precedence of poetry, and of showing
without saying. Finally, I could have shown them that mischaracterization, ·which is admittedly a kind of misdeed, can be committed only by
those who characterize, not by those who otherwise do. And who
among us does the characterizing? The lawyers, the judges, and even
more so the law teachers, we, who spend our professional speech in talk
of others' deeds. But most of the same law teachers whose misdeeds are
mischaracterizations also live exemplary lives, that contradict all their
misspoken teaching. My point is not to excuse mischaracterization, but
only to indicate more pointedly what is the mistake in mischaracterization: that of yielding to the intellect's empiricism, instead of returning
to the teachings of Philosophy. Of course doers have no such problem.
By the way, I verified this fact on my way at San Francisco International
Airport: no passengers would board airplanes whose pilots were adver-
tised as experts in the theory of flying. They dreaded the very thought
of a *Verstandesstaat*. These doers in fact loved wisdom, though very few
could state any philosophical law.

I could have said all this, and more, but without hesitation I took another tack. Echoes of the eleventh thesis on Feuerbach[37] were ringing in my ears, and I understood that my students needed only to grasp a marvelously simple thought: as H.L.A. Hart put it, "the assertion that [the Rule of Law] exists can only be an external statement of fact as an observer who did not accept the [R]ule might make and verify."[38] This language they spoke, hence there was hope. And then I knew what to say. Summoning all authority I was able to assume, I said: "Let us stop talking about Law. Let is rather go and do right. Then let us reassemble in this room, and you will see that, in your own life, the Rule of Law *was*." And by some miracle, that no rational faith would explain, they went out of the classroom with me. In that moment, they wrenched American law out of its futurity, made it a presence, and began to build a history that they would later contemplate with the pleasure one feels from the radiance of spirit.[39] For that moment (would it last?), and in their person, America became a state, and ceased to be the land of the future.

Now tell me. Did I answer them rightly?

---

37 "The philosophers have only *interpreted* the world, in various ways; the point is to *change* it." Karl Marx, *Early Writings* (Penguin Books, 1975), p. 423.

38 H.L.A. Hart, *supra,* note 7, p. 106.

39 A history for contemplation, not to be confused with the "history" of the objective science of historiography. See *supra,* note 8.

Toward A Critical Phenomenology
of Judging

Duncan Kennedy

The inquiry I propose here begins from a particular imagined point of view on the Rule of Law. I am going to imagine that I am a judge confronting a case that *at least initially* seems to present a conflict between "the law" and "how I want to come out."

I am not sure what difference it makes to the phenomenology of the Rule of Law that I begin with this situation rather than another. The whole experience of law may be sufficiently the same thing through and through so that wherever you start, you end up with approximately the same price. Or it may be that there is no experience of legality that's constant without regard to role and initial posture of the case. What I am convinced of is that you need to start with *some* particularization of the kind I've just sketched. I don't find myself at all convinced when people start out claiming they can tell us what the Rule of Law is without some such grounding in an imagined situation.

This judge is a U.S. District Court judge in Boston. I am from Boston. I'm more a ruling class elite type than a local politician or notable type, which is why I choose the federal forum. But what's most important is that the judge is responsible for *deciding* this case, rather than a party or an observer or an advocate. I am going to be looking at law as a person who will have to apply it, interpret it, change it, defy it, or whatever. I will do this in the context of the legal and lay community that follows what U.S.D.C. judges do, and with the possibility of appeal always present to my mind.

The more complex conditions of this inquiry have to do with the polarity between my initial impression of "the law" and my initial sense of how-I-want-to-come-out. What I want to do might be based on having been bribed and wanting to keep my bargain; or it might be based on a sense of what decision would be popular with my community (legal or local) or on what I thought the appeals court would likely do in the case of an appeal. It might be based on a sense that the equities of this particular case are peculiar because they favor an outcome different from what the law requires, even though the law is basically a very good one, and even though it was on balance a good decision to frame it so inflexibly that it couldn't adjust to take account of these particular equities.

Or it might be that I disagree with the way the law here resolves the problem of exceptional situations, believing that it could have been crafted to be flexible to take care of this case. Or it could be that I see the law here as "unfair" in the sense that, taking the whole rest of the system at face value, it would be better to change this rule. This rule might be an anomaly, etc. (Later we will take up the question of the rules about the judge changing the rules.)

Instead of any of these "I wants," imagine that I think the rule that seems to apply is bad because it strikes the wrong balance between two identifiable conflicting groups, and does so as part of a generally unjust overall arrangement that includes many similar rules, all of which ought in the name of justice to change. I mean to suggest a "political" objection to the law, and a how-I-want-to-come-out that is part of a general plan of opposition. This brings us close, I think, to the concern of the critics of critical legal studies.

Again, the experience of legality may well be different according to the character of the "I want" that opposes "the law". All I insist on is this: it is just useless to discuss the conflict of "personal preference vs. law" without specifying what kind of preference we are dealing with.

Here's what I mean by "my first impression that the law requires a particular outcome." Suppose that there is a strike of union bus drivers going on in Boston. The company hires non-union drivers and sets out to resume service. On the first day, union members lie down in the street outside the bus station to prevent the buses from passing. They do not disturb the general flow of traffic, and they are non-violent. The local police arrest them and cart them off, but this takes hours. They are charged with disturbing the peace and obstructing a public way (misdemeanors) and released on light bail. The next day other union members obstruct, with similar results. The buses run, but only late and amid a chaotic jumble. The company goes into federal court for an injunction against the union tactic.

When I first think about this case, not being a labor law expert, but having some general knowledge, I think, "There is no way they will be able to get away with this. The Rule of Law is going to be that workers cannot prevent the employer from making use of the buses during the strike. The company will get its injunction."

I disagree with this imagined rule. I don't think it should be the case that management can operate the means of production with substitute labor during a strike. I think there should be a rule that, until the dispute has been resolved, neither side can operate the means of production without the permission of the other (barring various kinds of extraordinary circumstances). This view is part of a general preference for transforming the current modes of American economic life in a direction of greater worker self-activity, worker control and management of enterprise, in a decentralized setting that blurs the lines between "owner" and "worker" and "public" and "private" enterprise.

My feeling that the law is against me in this case is a quick intuition about the way things have to be. I haven't actually read any cases or articles that describe what the employer can and can't do with the means of production [m.o.p.] during a strike. I vaguely remember "In Dubious Battle", a Steinbeck classic I read when I was 16. But I would bet money that some such rule exists.

If there is a rule that the employer can do what he wants with the m.o.p., I think it will probably turn out to be true that there is relief in federal court (under the rubric of unfair labor practices?). But I vaguely remember that federal courts aren't supposed to issue injunctions in labor disputes. If there is relief available, then I have a strong feeling that these workers have interfered with the employer's right to use the m.o.p. as he pleases during a strike, and that they threaten to continue to do so, and that they threaten irreparable injury to the employer, so that the employer can show the various things usually required to justify an injunction.

There are different elements of certainty and uncertainty here. I am quite sure the employer can use the m.o.p. as he pleases. I am not sure that the U.S.D.C. has jurisdiction under the labor law statutes to intervene on the employer's behalf when the local authorities are already enforcing the local general law about obstructing public ways. I am not sure that if there is a basis for federal intervention an injunction is appropriate. I will have to look into all these things before I'm really at all sure about how this case will or should come out.

On the other hand, I am *quite quite sure* that if there is a rule that the employer can use the m.o.p. any way he pleases during a strike, then the workers have violated it here. I am sure that what I mean by the rule is that the employer has both a privilege to act and a right to protection against interference. And I am also sure that what the workers did here *was* interference.

Since the supposed Rule of Law that I don't like won't get applied so as to lead to an injunction unless all the uncertainties are resolved against the workers, I do not yet confront a direct conflict between the law and how-I-want-to-come-out. But I do now already have the feeling of "the law" as a constraint on me. It's time to ask what that means.

The initial apparent objectivity of the objectionable rule. I use the word objectivity here to indicate that from my point of view the *application of the rule to this case* feels to me to be a non-discretionary, necessary, compulsory procedure. I can no more deny that, if there is such a rule, the workers have violated it, than I can deny that I am at this minute in Cambridge, MA, sitting on a chair, using a machine called a typewriter. The rule just applies itself. What I *meant* by interfering with the owner's use of the m.o.p. was workers lying down in the street when the employer tries to drive the buses out to resume service during the strike. I'm sure from the description that the workers actually intended to do exactly what the rule says they have no right to do.

Note that this sense of objectivity is internal—it's what happens in my head. There is a quite different question which will arise the minute I begin to think about the potential conflict between the law and how-I-want-to-come-out. How will other people see this case, supposing that the preliminary hurdles are overcome?

Sometimes it will seem to me that *anyone* (within the relevant universe) will react to this case as one where the rule applies. I imagine them going through the same process I did, and it is instantly obvious that they too will see the workers as having violated the rule. If this happens, the rule application acquires a double objectivity. The reaction of those other people is an anticipated fact like my anticipation that the sun will rise tomorrow or that a glass will break if I drop it on the floor.

It is important not to mush these forms of objectivity together. It is possible for me to see the case as "not clearly governed by the rule" when I do my interior rule application, but to anticipate that the relevant others will see it as "open and shut". And it is possible for me to see it as clear but to anticipate that others will see it as complex and confusing.

The next thing that happens is that I set to *work* on the problem of this case. I have already, as part of my life as I've lived it up to this moment, a set of intentions, a life-project as a judge, which will orient me among the many possible attitudes I could take to this work.

It so happens that I see myself as a political activist, someone with the "vocation of social transformation," as Roberto Unger put it. I see the set of rules in force as chosen by the people who had the power to make the choices in accord with their views on morality and justice and their own self interest, and I see the rules as remaining in force for no other reason than that no one has had the political vision and energy to change them. I see myself as a focus of political energy for change in an egalitarian, communitarian, decentralized, democratic socialist direction (which doesn't mean these slogans are any help in figuring out what the hell to do in any particular situation).

Given this general orientation, the work I am going to do in this case will have two objectives, which may or may not conflict. I want these specific workers to get away with obstructing the buses, and I want to change the law as much as possible in the direction of allowing workers a measure of legally legitimated control over the disposition of the m.o.p. during a strike.

If my only objective were to avoid an injunction against lying down in front of the buses during this strike, I would be tempted toward a strategy that would allow me to avoid altogether the apparent legal rule forbidding worker interference. I could just delay, in the hope that the workers will win the strike before I'm forced to rule. I could focus on developing a new version of the facts, and deny the injunction on that basis. I could rule on a "technicality" having no apparent substantive relevance (the statute of frauds, a mistake in the caption of a pleading).

On a much more substantive level, I could put my research energy into the issues of federal jurisdiction and the appropriateness of an injunction. Here, if the effort paid off, I might be able to change the law in a way favorable to workers in general, even though the change didn't formally address worker control over the m.o.p. during a strike.

But the strategy I want to discuss here is that of frontal assault on the application of the rule that the workers can't obstruct the company's use of the m.o.p. If I succeed, the result will be both to get the workers off in this case *and* to accomplish my law reform objective. There will be a small reduction in employer power to invoke the state apparatus, which will be practically useful in foreseeable future legal disputes over strikes. And the mantle of legal legitimacy will shift a little, from all out endorsement of management prerogatives to a posture that legitimates, to some degree, workers' claims to rights over the m.o.p.

What I see as interesting about the situation as I have portrayed it up to this point is that we are not dealing with a "case governed by a rule", but rather with a perception that a rule probably governs, and that applying the rule will very likely produce a particular (pro-company) result. The judge is neither free nor bound. I don't see it that way from *inside the situation*. From inside the situation, the question is where am I going to deploy the resources I have available for this case. The issue is how should I direct my *work* to bring about an outcome that accords with my sense of justice. My situation as a judge (initial perceived conflict between "the law" and how-I-want-to-come-out) is thus quite like that of a lawyer who is brought a case by a client and is afraid on first run-through that the client will lose. The question is, is this first impression one that will hold up as we set to work to develop the best possible case on the other side?

The situation of having to work to achieve an outcome is in my view fundamental to the situation of the judge. It is neither a matter of being bound nor a matter of being free. Or you could say that the judge is both free *and* bound. Free to deploy work in any direction, but limited by the pseudo-objectivity of the rule-as-applied, which he may or may not be able to overcome.

Isn't what I am doing illegitimate, from the standpoint of legality, right from the start? One could argue that since I think the law favors the company I have no business trying to develop the best possible case for the union. But this misunderstands the rules of the game of legality. All members of the community know that one's initial impression, that a particular rule governs, and that when applied to the facts it yields X result, is *often* wrong. That's what makes law such a trip. What at first looked open and shut is ajar, and what looked vague and altogether indeterminate abruptly reveals itself to be quite firmly settled under the circumstances. So it is an important part of the judges' and the lawyers' role that they are to test whatever conclusions they have reached about "the correct legal outcome" by trying to develop the best possible argument on the other side. In my role as an activist judge I am just doing what I'm supposed to do when I test my first impression against the best pro-union argument I can develop. What would betray legality would be to adopt the wrong attitude at the *end* of the reasoning process, when I've reached a *conclusion* about "what the law requires" and find it still in conflict with how-I-want-to-come-out.

For the moment, I'm free to play around.

The euphoric moment in which I conceive legal reasoning as "playing around with the rule" doesn't last long. What follows is panic, as I rack my brain for *any* way around the overwhelming sense that if the rule is "workers can't interfere with the owner's use of the m.o.p. during a strike," then we have a loser on our hands. There is an element of shame to this panic: it's not just that I'm not coming up with anything; I also feel that I *should* be coming up with something. It's a disgrace—it shows I lack legal reasoning ability. I feel like a fool for trumpeting the indeterminacy of doctrine and claiming to be a manipulative whizz.

As my panic deepens, I begin to consider alternatives. If I can't mount an attack on the rule-as-applied, maybe I will have to research the earlier contract between the union and the bus company. I have a strong feeling that contracts are manipulable, using concepts like good faith, implication of terms, and the public interest, which is relevant here. Maybe I'll have to try to "read something in". But this is clearly *less good* than going right for the rule itself.

Then I start thinking about the federal injunction aspect of this, as opposed to the labor tort aspect. I'm sure that the combination of the 1930s anti-injunction statute with federal court injunctive enforcement of at least some terms in collective bargaining agreements (after *Lincoln Mills*? I can't quite remember) must have made a total hash of the question of when federal courts will grant injunctions. I think longingly that if only I could worry just about *that*, I bet I could *easily* come up with a good pro-worker argument. But that line is also *less good* than going for the rule.

Then there are the really third-rate solutions of hoping the facts will turn out to be at least arguably different than they seemed to be when I first heard about the case, and that the company's lawyers will make a stupid technical mistake.

All the while, I'm desperately racking my brains. I think I have good maxims for legal reasoning, but what are they? There are *always* exceptions to the rule, but I can't think of any here. The rule represents a compromise between two conflicting policies, so there must be a grey area where the terms of the compromise are not clear.

When an idea starts to come, it just comes, little by little getting clearer as I work to tease it out, flesh it out, add analogies. Here it is:

Of course (oh, that reassuring "of course" at the beginning of the argument, how I love to feel it tripping off my tongue), it is not *literally* true that the workers are forbidden from "interfering with the owners' use of the m.o.p. during a strike." They can picket, and use all kinds of publicity measures to dissuade people from riding the company's buses.

Here I begin to lose my grip again. Clearly, lying down in the roadway is a far cry from picketing, which doesn't interfere at all *physically* with the company's use of the buses and is after all justified as an exercise of First Amendment rights to free speech. This exception won't do me any good.

After more false leads and panic (I try manipulating the concept of "owner" to get the workers a piece of the action, but that just seems to push into the inferior implied contract route) I come back to my exception. The workers did lie down in the street to block the buses, but they did not intend to and did not in fact use force to prevent them from rolling. After all, they submitted peacefully to arrest. And the press was everywhere. Obviously the worker on the ground *could not have* physically prevented the bus from rolling, because it could have rolled right over him.

Still, the company failed on these two days of lie-ins to resume service in the fashion it had planned. The workers did physically obstruct the owner's use of the means of production and were delighted to do so. It wasn't just a side effect.

On the other hand, maybe we argue that this was a symbolic protest, an attempt to: (a) exert moral suasion on the company by impressing it with the extreme feeling of the workers and their willingness to take risks, their sense that the company is *theirs* as much as management's; and (b) a gesture toward the public through the media.

I will emphasize the non-violent civil disobedience aspect: a physical tactic that *could not in fact* have prevented the use of the m.o.p. by the company, and submission to arrest.

I could hold that because of these factors there should be no federal labor law injunctive remedy beyond what is accorded under state law (narrow version). Or that this is the exercise of first amendment rights so that *injunction of a non-violent civil disobedient protest* would be an unconstitutional restriction of expression, even though it is of course perfectly permissible for the state to arrest the demonstrators and subject them to its normal criminal process (broad version).

By this time, I'm getting high. I have no idea whether this line of argument will work. I have even lost track a little of exactly how this argument can be brought to bear in the company's federal court action for an injunction. (This is probably because I've gotten into my holding on the merits before clarifying in my own mind what the basis of federal jurisdiction may be, and before getting into the anti-junction Wagner Act issue.) But I am nonetheless delighted. My heart lifts because it *seems* that the work of legal reasoning within my pro-worker project is paying off.

What I've tried to do here is to turn this into a first amendment (or at least a "free speech policy") case. I relied on the idea that there had to be *some* limit to the employer's freedom from interference, came up with picketing by trying to imagine what the workers certainly *could* do to him, and then looked for an extension of the picketing idea to embrace the particular facts of this case.

Another way to put it is that I stopped imagining the rule of "no interference" as the only thing out there—as dominating an empty field and therefore grabbing up and incorporating any new fact situation that had anything at all "sort of like interference" in it. I tried to find the (affirmative other) rules that set the limits of this one, so I could tuck my case under their wing. Once I identified those other affirmative rules (protecting picketing and other first-amendment-based attacks on the employer's use of the m.o.p.), I restated the facts of the lie-in to emphasize those aspects that fit (non-violence, submission to arrest, one prone body can't stop a Sceni-cruiser unless the Sceni-cruiser wants to be stopped).

The minute I get rolling, new wrinkles occur to me. Maybe we should see this as an appeal by union workers to the non-union replacement bus drivers. It is *they*, not the union members, who actually stop the buses on the street and fail thereby to carry out the company's plan to resume service. It would be ok to try to persuade the non-union replacements with flyers, to picket them, to threaten them with anger and non-association and guilt trip them and swear at them. This is just a small extension of those tactics. It is a physical statement to them. Will this fly? I have no idea. It is part of the brainstorming process, rather than a deduction of the rule that covers the case. It is part of the work of producing lots of alternative ways at the problem, hoping that one of them will break through. I am already wondering whether it's even worth the time to pursue this one further.

The question is not whether my off-the-wall first legal intuitions turn out to be right. They may eventually generate at least superficially plausible legal arguments. But maybe it will turn out that the law is so well settled in another direction that I will have to abandon them and try something else the minute I get out *Gorman on Labor Law* and *Prosser on Torts*. What I'm asking is that you focus on the process of legal reasoning viewed as a kind of work with a purpose, the purpose here being to make the case come out the way my sense of justice tells me it ought to, in spite of what seems at first like the *resistance* or *opposition* of "the law".

Resistance or opposition is the characteristic of the law when I anticipate it as a constraint on how-I-want-to-come-out. But if my initial sense had been that the law was "on my side", it would be a resistance or opposition from the point of view of the company. I would experience it as a protective barrier I was building around my position, perhaps, or as armour I need to fit to my particular body so that the other side won't be able to strip it away or penetrate it. If I had no sense of "which way the law goes on this," so that each side had an equal opportunity to make a persuasive legal argument, I might experience the law as a body of raw material out of which to "build my case", or perhaps as a mass of wet clay that two opposing potters are each trying to shape before it hardens.

The image changes according to how the law initially presents itself in relation to how-I-want-to-come-out. But in each case I am suggesting that we experience law as a medium in which one pursues a project, rather than as something that tells us what we have to do. Law constrains as a physical medium constrains—you can't do absolutely anything you want with a pile of bricks, and what you can do depends on how many you have, as well as on your other circumstances. In this sense, that you are building something out of a given set of bricks constrains you, controls you, deprives you of freedom.

On the other hand, the constraint a medium imposes is relative to your freely chosen project—to your choice of what you want to make. The medium doesn't tell you what to do with it—that you *must* make the bricks into a little doghouse rather than into a garden wall. In the same sense, I am free to work in the legal medium to justify the workers' actions against the company. How my argument will look in the end will depend in a fundamental way on the legal materials—rules, cases, policies, social stereotypes, historical images—but this dependence is a far cry from the determination of the outcome by a process of legal argument that could only be done correctly in one way.

The introduction of the metaphor of a physical medium does not help us solve the problem of just how constraining the law is. All it does is suggest that we should understand both freedom and constraint as aspects of the experience of work—freely chosen project constrained by material properties of the medium—rather than thinking in the back of our mind of a transcendentally free subject who "could do anything", contrasted with a robot programmed by the law.

One might accept the notion that legal argument is manipulation of the legal materials understood as a medium, and still believe that the medium constrains very tightly. An absolutely basic question is whether there are some outcomes that you just can't reach so long as you obey the internal rules of the game of legal reasoning. These would be "things you just can't make with bricks", or silk purses you can't make with this particular sow's ear. Or, on the other hand, it might be the case that the medium is more like watercolors, or oil paint, or music, so that we could say that you can represent *anything* in the medium, however imperfectly. (The musical version of the Alps may be harder to connect up with your touristic experience than the realistic painting on the postcard.)

Make any assumption you want as to how tightly the medium constrains the message. Perhaps there is only one correct legal result in most cases, or perhaps it is just that there are some results sometimes that you can't reach through correct legal reasoning. I am not going to discuss that traditional political science-jurisprudence question, just because that question is always put in terms of the sharp opposition of discretion versus control, albeit sometimes the two are mixed or combined.

What I want to ask is *how*, rather than how *tightly* law constrains when we understand it as a medium through which my liberal-activist-judge self pursues social justice. When we are clearer about this, it will be time to ask whether it is ever (or sometimes, or always) possible in the last analysis to have a conflict between the law and how-I-want-to-come-out, and, if so, what the ethics of the conflict may be.

My model of constraint is that people—me as a judge—want to back up their statement of a preference for an outcome—the workers should not be enjoined—with an argument to the effect that to enjoin the workers would "violate the law". I don't think we can understand how this desire to legalize my position constrains me without saying something about why I want to do it.

First, I see myself as having promised some diffuse public that I will decide according to law, and it is clear to me that a *minimum* meaning of this pledge is that I won't do things for which I don't have a good legal argument. (This says nothing, as I have said, about just how tightly this promise constrains me as to the merits.)

Second, various people in my community will sanction me severely if I offer no good legal argument for my action. It is not just that I may be reversed and will have broken my promise. It is also that both friends and enemies will see me as having violated a role constraint that they approve of (for the most part), and they will make me feel their disapproval of my conduct.

Third, I want my position to stick. Although I am free to decide the case any way I want in the sense that no one will physically prevent me from entering a decree for either side, I am not free, but rather bound by the appellate court's reaction. I believe that by developing a strong legal argument I will make it dramatically less likely that my outcome will be reversed.

Fourth, by engaging in legal argument I can shape the outcomes of future cases and of popular consciousness about what kinds of action are legitimate—as here, for example, I can marginally influence what people think about worker interference with the m.o.p. during a strike.

Fifth, every case is part of my life-project of being a liberal-activist judge. What I do in this case will affect my ability to do things in other cases, enhancing and/or diminishing my legal and political credibility as well as my technical reputation with the various constituencies that will notice.

Sixth, since I see legal argument as a branch of ethical argument, I would like to know for my own ethical purposes how my position looks translated into this particular ethical medium.

I could achieve some of these objectives all of the time and most of them some of the time without engaging in the kind of direct challenge that I described above to my first adverse intuition about the law. I could, for example, acknowledge that the law favors the company and refuse to grant the injunction as an act of civil disobedience, and then take the consequences. Or I might cheat and lie, for example, by mis-stating the facts so thoroughly that there would no longer appear to be any case of interference with the company's property.

Each alternative has costs and dangers. I don't want to be absolute about it, since I can conceive situations in which I think I would go quite unhesitatingly for a non-substantive approach. But there will be many, many situations in which it appears that, if I wish to achieve my listed goals, the only way or the obviously best way is to try legal argument.

As soon as I set out to do some legal argument, I experience the law-medium as internally differentiated, and indeed as highly structured. It is that structure that I will work to change into a configuration favorable to how I want to come out. I have already given an extremely simplified example of the process. In the lie-in case, I restated one general rule to constrict its scope, while simultaneously restating the facts to get them out from its domain into that of the counter-rule that the First Amendment affirmatively protects some activities that interfere with the employer's use of the m.o.p. during a strike.

The imagery of the facts of the case as located, though moveable by restatement, and as located on one side or the other of a boundary separating the domains of two general rules, can be extended when we add other cases, with their own facts and their manipulable holdings, and policies. We can understand the law medium as a field, in which principles have boundaries, delimited by decided cases as points, and by their holdings extending to cover other boundary cases. Policies we can see as vectors of force in the field, equilibrated at boundaries, but with one vector dominating another on either side. I don't have time here to develop this mode of description in any detail. But the basic point is that the different elements we use in legal argument are a configuration, which we grasp initially in a gestalt process, and which we can work to rearrange.

A basic condition of this restating or rearranging or manipulating activity is that its difficulty varies from case to case. There is variation in the "obviousness gap" between how I want to come out and how I imagined others think the case "obviously" ought to come out if we "just applied existing law". Where the obviousness gap is large, there are large risks and large potential benefits from working out a legal argument that convinces my audience that their first impression was wrong. The judge's store of legal legitimacy, of *mana*, will either be depleted or increased depending on whether he persuades, or merely seems to have gone through an argumentative charade.

The work of trying to overcome the obviousness gap will be different according to the configuration of the field. Some fields might be described as impacted, meaning that they initially present themselves as highly organized. Boundaries are long straight lines picked out with many cases each referring in its holding to the other cases and indicating how the remaining gaps should be filled; policies are articulated and "easy" cases well within the boundaries have been decided as such. The impacted field is the image of legal necessity, and if I want to decide my case in a way that seems to disorder it, I will have to work hard to overcome the obviousness gap.

This problem will be dramatically less severe if the case presents itself as "of first impression", meaning that the field virtually announces a gap, conflict or ambiguity. In such a case, it will be expected that I must be "creative", either in the way of the great case or in that of penny ante judicial rule elaboration. Somewhere in between these two poles, I may confront an unrationalized field, begging for a "strong" opinion bringing order out of chaos, or a contradictory field (think of the state-action doctrine, or regulatory-takings doctrine, or promissory estoppel, or unfair competition) in which the scatter of cases makes it possible to claim that *any* fact pattern raises basic policy issues.

There is an ideal scenario in which I am able to represent the legal field so that the law corresponds exactly to how-I-want-to-come-out. What was initially an impacted field with the lie-in unequivocally prohibited (an easy case) becomes, to the surprise of my public, an impacted field in which the lie-in is a case that is clearly permitted (or at least not enjoinable). I close a large obviousness gap by a field manipulation that is notably elegant—a dramatic change in outcome with surprisingly little disturbance of the elements of the field.

When it happens that way, I feel euphoria, indeed a moment of dangerous omnipotence, delight at the plasticity of the natural/social field-medium and narcissistic ecstasy at the favorable reaction of my public (not to speak of sober joy at all the good I will be able to do with my increased credibility). But before you put me down as an egotist, I want to add that *some* element of this pleasure is quite legitimate. I had an intuition about the justice of the situation—how-I-wanted-to-come-out in this case was in accord with an intuition that the law as I initially apprehended it was unfair to a particular group. If I have succeeded in making the law fairer to that group, my pleasure will be in part an altruistic emotion that seems to me no cause for shame: I will have helped out.

Too bad it doesn't always turn out that way.

I will try to describe below some of the ways things don't turn out ideally. But first dwell for a bit on my uncertainty, as I begin my argument, about what will happen during its course. I *will* have an initial estimate, a guess about how large the obviousness gap is, about the resources I will have to engage in order to overcome it, and about the chances that I will fall short to one degree or another. But why can't I tell in advance the more or less precise dimensions of my problem, the means at my disposal, and the quality of my solution? I don't know *why*. But here is *how* I don't know in advance, how this form of work resembles the work of making a handsome, well-functioning building more than it resembles what we think of as "strictly technical" or "engineering" problems, in which, it seems, we can achieve a high degree of advance knowledge of what the outcome of the work will be.

Projection. I know as I begin my argument that I may have misjudged the way the field will look to other people. I'm not trying to persuade myself, but rather some hypothetical public. But I have to construct their way of seeing it on the basis of my own vision. In my own case, it often happens that the field looks at first glance to be at least unrationalized and very possibly contradictory, when others see it as at least close to impacted. In other words, I have a bias, measured by the vision of others, toward seeing the field as underdetermined, as unstructured, as open to all kinds of manipulation. Remember that my initial apprehension of the configuration of the field is a gestalt process, very firmly located in the eye of the beholder, however dependent on stimuli that are external. Other people seem to me to see the field as *always* impacted, and adversely at that, until they have put an inordinate amount of pain into loosening it up.

Virtu. The skill of legal argument is to close a big obviousness gap with minimal disturbance of the elements of the field. It is the skill of combining the different moves—restating facts and holdings and rules and policies and stereotypes—in such a way as to achieve multiple goals at minimal cost. There is no way to be sure you will be able to do this the next time you try. How much you can change the field through argument is a property of *yours*, that is, is determined by your skill, as well as a property of the field, but the property of yours is unknowable in advance. There is such a thing as a good day and such a thing as a bad day. Internal psychic factors like adrenalin, panic, fatigue, but also internal factors that seem random, or psycho-analytically knowable only after the fact, all impinge. Hey, life is a gamble, here as everywhere else.

Hidden properties. My initial apprehension of the field just doesn't tell me that much about it. An analogy is my initial apprehension of a body of water through which I am going to navigate a boat. I can see the surface of the water but usually not what lies beneath it. Yet there are lots and lots of signs on the surface of what is beneath. Some people are terrific at "reading" the surface; others not so good. But no matter how good you are at reading, there is lots that is just not knowable in advance. In legal argument, I have no way of knowing with any precision what is contained in the thousands of cases I haven't read that might be relevant to my problem, or in the thousands of other kinds of legal materials scattered across creation waiting to be put to use here.

The consequence of these different kinds of uncertainty is that I can never know in advance whether it will be possible to develop a legal argument for how-I-want-to-come-out that will persuade any part of my audience. Sometimes, this feels obvious from the start. I never break through my initial panicked sense that this is a case the workers can't possibly win. It sometimes happens that my sense that they can't possibly win emerges slowly as I pursue what at first seemed like a promising course of argument.

Sometimes it's less dramatic than running up against the brick wall of the experienced objectivity of the rule. Maybe it turns out that I can make an argument that is "plausible", but won't actually convince many people; or that I can convince my audience that the law is a lot more favorable to the workers than they thought, but not so favorable as to prohibit an injunction of this particular illegal action. Maybe I can confuse the issue, so to speak, by successfully shooting down the employer's arguments, without establishing a killer argument on my side, so that the case now appears to be one of first impression which "could have come out either way, depending on what judge you got, and you happened to get Kennedy, who we all know is pro-worker anyway." Another possibility is a sharp break between what I think of as good legal argument and what I think will please my audience. I may come up with a field-manipulation that strikes me as clumsy or just plain wrong—one that wouldn't convince me for a minute of anything—but which I think will appeal to this public as highly plausible.

I experience the course of events as contingent. I don't have, and I know I don't have, a technique for predicting with a high degree of certainty what will happen to my first impression of conflict between the law and how-I-want-to-come-out. I can only find out the actual posture of the law by going through the work of argument. When I've finished, I'll be able to tell you what happened. My story will represent what happened as the necessary consequence of the latent properties of the field and of my level of skill, but this will be very much an after-the-fact reconstruction. While it's happening, the situation seems to open toward a multiplicity of possible outcomes, none of which would violate any strongly held theoretical tenets.

Even after the fact, I won't know exactly why it turned out that I couldn't budge the field. In particular (I think this is an important aspect of judging that no one has focussed on) I won't know whether my failure to develop a plausible legal argument for non-injunction of the lie-in was a consequence of my own failure to correctly perceive and manipulate the field, or, by contrast, a consequence of the "inherent properties of the field", so that there was nothing I could have done. Did I screw up, or was I doomed from the start?

Of course we are not in a condition of total ignorance about the failure. For example, next week another judge or lawyer might produce an argument against enjoining the lie-in that was highly plausible, and dissolved the felt objectivity of the rule against interference with the employer's use of the m.o.p., at least as applied to this case. If that happened, I would say to myself, with a lot of confidence, that my failure last week was a failure of skill rather than something preordained by the latent structure of the law-field. Or I might discover a whole series of earlier unsuccessful attempts to argue the case convincingly, and conclude that my failure was not so shameful after all.

Knowledge of this kind is not inconsistent with the sense of radical contingency I am asserting here. It can be shown that my failure was a failure of skill when someone else does what I couldn't do, and there is suggestive evidence in the failure of others that my failure was a consequence of the properties of the field. But it's *never* possible to prove convincingly *from the inside* that there was just no way to make it fly. You can't prove it couldn't be done.

I have had many times the initial apprehension of the objective coverage of a case by a rule. I have many times started out thinking, "no way". And I have many times had the experience of the apparent objectivity dissolving under the pressure of the work of legal argument. I have no theory that tells me in advance when that will happen and when it won't. I just have to try and see. When it doesn't work, sometimes someone else can do it. And sometimes I come back to the problem later and succeed where before I seemed to fail through no fault of my own. *From the inside*, what happens to my initial experience of the rule as objective is just radically contingent.

I can *imagine* what it would be like to be able to tell in advance whether or not the rule's objective self-application will stand the test of time and effort. I can *imagine* having a technique, like the technique of a surveyor, say, that would tell me with great confidence that if I extend a bridge's span at a particular angle in a particular direction it will eventually hit the other side of the ravine at a predetermined spot. But that's just not the way it is in legal argument, at least for me. And in all honesty I have to say that people who think differently turn out, in my experience, to be ignorant.

The normative power of the field. Through the whole discussion to this point, I have spoken as a judge who knows how he wants to come out and is vigorously trying to bring the law into accord. Sometimes I apprehend the law as plastic and co-operative, sometimes as resistant or even adamant, but I and my favored outcome are always the same. It is now time to critique the how-I-want-to-come-out pole of our duality. First, however, lets reify it with an acronym: HIWTCO.

HIWTCO is not a datum given externally, something that comes into the picture from outside. HIWTCO is *relative to the field*. This is true in the weak sense that I have decided HIWTCO in response to a question posed in terms of the existing social universe which includes law. I don't want these particular workers, living in our particular society under a particular set of legal rules to be enjoined from lying-in. I can't even formulate HIWTCO without referring to this legal context to give that result a meaning.

But HIWTCO is relative to the law field in a much more interesting and important way than this. I've been treating the law field as though it were a physical medium, say clay or bricks, when what it is in fact is a set of declarations by other people (possibly including an earlier me) about how ethically serious people ought to respond to situations of conflict. As I manipulate the field, I am reading and re-reading these declarations, apparently addressed to me, and trying to absorb their messages about what I ought to do. Indeed, before I ever heard of this case, I was already knowledgeable about hundreds and hundreds of opinions by judges and lawyers and legislators about how to handle conflicts roughly analogous to this one.

As a preliminary matter this means that we are *not* dealing with a confrontation between "my gut feeling about the case" and the law, unless we understand my "gut" as an organ deeply conditioned by existence in our legalized universe. I simply don't have intuitions about social justice that are independent of my knowledge of what judges and legislators have done in the past about situations like the one before me. Other actors in the legal system have influenced, persuaded, outraged, puzzled, and instructed me, until I can never be sure in what sense an opinion I strongly hold is "really" mine rather than theirs. I don't even think such a question has an answer.

But the more important point is that my initial impression of conflict between the law and HIWTCO may disappear because HIWTCO changes, as well as because I manage to change the law. Further, the very resistance of the law to change in the direction of HIWTCO may impell HIWTCO to change in the direction of the law. I may find myself persuaded by my study of the materials that my initial apprehension of HIWTCO was wrong. I may find that I now want to come out the way I initially perceived the law coming out. This is what I mean by the normative power of the field.

<u>Who is the field</u>? I try to move the law in the direction of HIWTCO, and to the extent the law is resistant, I find HIWTCO under pressure to move toward the law. But neither HIWTCO nor the law field are physical objects. If I experience "pressure" as I read through the legal materials, if the very fact of my initial apprehension that the law favors the employer exerts pressure, it is because the field is a message rather than a thing. It is a message of a kind I'm familiar with, a message of a kind I've dealt with before. Indeed, I am one of the authors of the message.

Precedents come to me as little stories called fact situations that judges resolved in particular ways. What they did interests me in the way an earlier painter's work might interest a later painter. But interest is too weak a word. Especially when they are put together in patterns, precedents reveal possibilities that it would have have taken me a long time to come up with, or that I might never have come up with at all. I look at six outcomes, and I say to myself:

> Oh, they devised a strategy of banning all picketing, but allowing just about any
> kind of secondary boycott. Hmm. I wonder why. Oh, I get it, they had a rough
> distinction between physically confrontive and non-confrontive tactics. Or
> maybe they were particularly concerned with freedom not to contract in the
> boycott cases, and were worried about the implications for business combina-
> tions of banning labor combinations.

Just studying these patterns may change my view because the study
will set my mind going in directions that otherwise wouldn't have happened. But there is also the elemental normative power of any outcome
reached by people I identify with. Because I think they were up to the
same thing I am up to, *whatever* they came up with has in its favor an
initial sense that it's probably what I would have come up with too.

I place my lie-in in the field among the various precedents, as more
of an interference than individual picketing, etc. Immediately, the analog-
ical weight of the precedents pulls me toward wanting to come out as
"the law" would have me come out. Given what I know about what
they were up to, by inference from the way they came out in those cases,
I think they would have come out as follows in this case. If they would
have come out that way, then since I am like them I will probably want
to come out that way too. This is the first-order-normative power of the
field.

The second-order-normative power of the field comes from the fact
that all these judges (and others) have left us more than just a record of
fact situations and outcomes. There are all the overtly normative explanations of outcomes by reference to rules and policies. There are hundreds
of particular statements about *why* we should come out in a particular
way under particular circumstances, sometimes very particularly defined
circumstances, but sometimes how we should come out in large classes
of fact situations quite abstractly defined (for example, the workers can't
interfere with the owner's use of the m.o.p. during a strike).

Now the practice of recording outcomes for fact situations, along
with messages about why those outcomes are ethically and politically
and legally correct, is no great mystery to me, since I do it all the time.
I know first hand what it means to try to indicate for the future how
some future dispute should be resolved, and I have a good idea of what
it is like to succeed. The person you've tried to influence says to you
something like:

> I had this problem, and I wondered what you would have to say about it, so I
> looked up your decision in the X case, where you gave your theory of what
> disruptive tactics labor should be permitted to use during a strike, and I found

it very helpful. In fact, you might say what I did in the Y case was try to apply your theory. Of course, you may think I botched it completely.

I believe that it is possible to record messages about how to deal with future situations that will be intelligible to actors in the future, and that it is possible for those actors to set out to "follow" the messages or directions, and that sometimes they do actually do something that is well described as "following the message". I sometimes feel that the people who laid down all these messages that together make up the field had the case before me in mind, and intended to instruct me to resolve it in a particular way.

To get to the second-order-normative power of the field, they have to be telling me not only that this is the rule *they* would apply, and here's how to apply it, but also that it is the *right* rule, that it is the *way I ought to come out*. The normative power of the field at this second order comes from the fact that I identify with these ought-speakers. I respect them. I honor them. When they speak, I listen. I even tremble if I think I am going against their collective wisdom. They are members of the same community working on the same problems. They are *old*; they are *many*. They are steeped in a tradition of serious ethical inquiry whose power I have felt on countless occasions, a tradition that seems to me a partially valid great accomplishment of the otherwise cruddy civilization of which I am a tiny part.

It is no good telling me that my reverence for the messages of these ancients is "irrational". It's not a question of rationality. When I read their words, it is as though I myself were talking. (Of course, when I'm reading my own earlier opinions, it *is* me in an earlier incarnation that's talking.) I am not able to treat these ethical pronouncements about how to decide cases like this one as though they were a set of randomly generated possible answers to a math problem. In that case, I test each answer "coldly", so to speak, without any investment at all in its correctness or incorrectness. But as I sit reading the messages of the ancients about cases like this one (or even, I may sometimes feel with horror, about this very case neatly anticipated) I can't remain neutral. I want them to agree with me. And I want to agree with them. I feel I *ought* to agree with them.

In this state of mind, I may discover that I can adopt the voice of the ancients, know what they are talking about when they extol the sacredness of owner's rights, and that what they are saying actually accurately expresses something that I think too. I set out to manipulate the field so that the law would favor the lie-in, but in order to do that I have to enter into the discourse of law. In the process I have to undergo its intimate prestige. I discover that I know what they were talking about because I myself am capable of thinking just what they thought. At that point, the normative force of the field is just one side in an interior discussion between my divided selves about who really should win this case anyway.

The messages that constitute the field are on one level just a set of verbal formulae. On another, they are speech I imaginatively impute to the "ancients". On a third level, the resistance of the field is just another name for my ambivalence about whether or not I should enjoin the lie-in. To the question "who is the field"? the answer has ultimately to be that the field is me, resisting myself.

Conversion. It is possible that I will resolve my ambivalence by just adopting the field as I initially apprehended it as a correct ethical statement as well as a correct perception of what the law is. In other words, I will find that I no longer want to come out against an injunction, but rather that my intuition of social justice is now that an injunction ought to issue, just as I initially thought the law required. But this is only one of many possible modes of interaction and ultimate equilibration of the law and HIWTCO. Here are some of the other possibilities.

I move the law and the law moves me. The outcome may be a modification of HIWTCO that brings it into accord with a new view of the field, one substantially different from my initial apprehension. Such a compromise might involve conceding that *these* workers went too far, though the law will not enjoin *all* lie-ins. Or it might involve not enjoining *these* workers, but conceding that my initial pro lie-in position went much too far, so the workers better not take the next step they appear to be contemplating.

A compromise, like a restatement of the law to correspond to HIWTCO, or conversion of HIWTCO to correspond to the law, has the peculiarity of *resolving* the initial perceived conflict. But this may not happen. The law may move me, and I may move the law, but they may end up still in conflict, albeit *less* in conflict. It's also possible that the normative pull of the field will leave me confused or ambivalent, where I had earlier been quite clear about HIWTCO. Or the reverse might happen, with a vague sense of HIWTCO clarified through the imagined dialogue with the ancients. As always, from inside the practice of legal argument the outcome is radically indeterminate.

How it sometimes doesn't work. What I have just described might be called the counter-ideal to the scenario in which I manipulate the law-field to correspond to HIWTCO. Here, the law field manipulates

HIWTCO, stimulating first ambivalence and then perhaps outright conversion to the other side. But the field is no more necessarily normatively powerful than I am necessarily manipulatively powerful.

To have normative power, the field must present itself as objectively favoring an outcome. Since normative power resides in the voice of the ancients, which is also just the voice of my ambivalent other half, I must be able to "read" the field in order to feel its power. The field must present itself as at least somewhat impacted, rather than as unrationalized, collapsed, contradictory or loopified. What I mean by those configurations is just that I can't integrate the cacophony of different speaking ancients into a single voice with a message. The disordered fields may influence me, in the sense that after exposure to them HIWTCO changes in one direction or another. But they are not exercising normative power, by which I persist in meaning the power to persuade me to a view that you are trying to persuade me to.

But even supposing I have an initial sense of how the law comes out that I can contrast with HIWTCO, it does not follow that the field will exercise normative power. The message I apprehend as "the law" is at several removes from a conviction of my own about what I want to do. It is a message I have to decode, rather than a thought immediately accessible to me inside my own mind (without making too much of the mediate/immediate distinction). There will always be an element of mystery as to whose message it is, whether I have properly understood it, whether it is "applicable" here at all. Until I "make it my own" and begin to argue the side of the law against HIWTCO, the message hovers between the life I can give it and the status of dead formula.

The message is from the past, from people who put it together in the past (including my past self, if I was involved). Even if I can understand it and enter into it, it is yesterday's newspaper, queer looking because so much has happened that it doesn't and couldn't take into account. The message is that the field was not developed by a clairvoyant as a message to the future; it is the product of judges deciding cases and writing opinions to deal with their problems, though with an eye toward the shape of the field for future cases. The way we constructed the field dates it and thereby deprives it of the normative bit it would have if it spoke in the voice of someone looking over my shoulder as I study the facts of the lie-in.

The message was composed by other people, though I may have played a small part myself. I conceded above that just about *any* message I can understand will have *some* normative power, if it is a normative message. That I can understand it all means that there was another person out there thinking about this problem, with that degree of community with me that mere personhood is alone enough to establish. From that communal identification, however limited it may be, comes the power to move me just by saying "you ought to do thus and so." But there are others and then there are others.

I will interpret the field as a message from particular others of a particular historical moment, and, as I particularize, I find myself less and less convinced. The architects of the law of labor relations I apprehend as applicable here were turn-of-the-century conservative state court judges, and New Deal reformers. I have mixed feelings about both groups and about the legal strategies of which these by-ways of labor law form a part. My experience of the normative pull of the field on HIWTCO is not like my experience of the pull of gravity on my body. My own interpretive construction of the message and its senders seems, at least, to have a great effect on how and how strongly I feel the normative pull. (Gravity may just be a weaker case—who these days will affirm the reality of the physical universe?)

What determines HIWTCO? From inside the practice of legal argument, the only possible answer to this question is that I determine the outcome of the interaction between my initial apprehension of the law field and my initial intuition of HIWTCO. I determine HIWTCO. As I develop the case against an injunction of the lie-in, I am restating, and therefore I am also stating the law about lie-ins. At some point, I may "get the message" of that law, and find myself developing it in my own mind as an argument against the position I have been taking, against HIWTCO. Then at some point I may find that "I am changing my mind," and then that "I have changed my mind."

It is a little hard to figure out what it means to have an "I" inside me who is capable of changing or not changing a "my mind" that is both the same as that "I" and different enough so that "I" can determine it rather than just *being* it. But it is true to my experience to say that HIWTCO is undetermined right up to the moment when something has happened that moots the question. I could always change my mind about HIWTCO, and I have on occasion found myself changing my mind *very* late in the game. I decide how I want to come out under the influence of the normative power of a field whose configuration I have reconstituted for myself under the pressure of how I want to come out. Sometimes this dialectic closes to a legal argument that I believe in and that convinces others. Sometimes the outcome is less felicitous, and I am left with confusion or flat conflict, when the moment to *do something* arrives. Then I have to do something—to civilly disobey, withdraw, decide against my intuition of justice, or write a disingenuous opinion. What should it be? I think, as I have said already, that "it all depends," but that is for another paper.

Imagine that you are a professor of jurisprudence, in possession of professional knowledge of the nature of law. Suppose that you approach me in my dark cloud of ignorance of whether or not I will be able to overcome the gap between the law and how-I-want-to-come-out. You argue that legal rules, like the rule that the workers can't interfere with the owner's use of the m.o.p. during a strike, *never* determine the outcomes of cases. And since the legal rules are the only things that stand in the way of my coming out the way I want to come out, I have no problem. Legal theory indicates that I am home free, or at least that I ought to be home free. If I'm not, it's because I've failed at legal argument, not because of any properties inherent to the field I'm trying to manipulate.

In my role of humble law-artificer, you can expect me to ask you how you can be so sure. You might respond that since Wittgenstein we know that no rule can determine the scope of its own application. It follows more or less directly (unless you insist on a detour through semiotics, structuralism and deconstruction) that the mere statement, "the workers can't interfere with the owner's use of the m.o.p. during a strike," tells us *nothing* about whether or not they can lie-in to block substitute workers from driving the buses out of the garage onto the great American highway. There is a whole work of interpretation, inherently subjective and indeed perhaps even inherently arbitrary (from the standpoint of my humble artificer's idea of reason), that we have to go through to get from the rule to "the facts". And "of course" the facts aren't any more "just there" than the rule.

My experience with legal argument doesn't allow me to meet your jurisprudential position on its own ground. What I can say as a legal arguer is that sometimes I come up against the rule as a felt objectivity, and can't budge it. This doesn't mean that I agree with it, or that I think anyone would necessarily condemn me if I disregarded or changed it. All it means is that I say to myself, "here's the rule that applies to this case," "we all know that this is the rule," and "here's how it applies," and "everyone is going to apply it that way."

I am perfectly aware that the rule is not a physical object, and that deciding how to apply it involves a social, hence in some sense a subjective process. But there is this procedure I've performed many times in my mind, in many different contexts, of applying a rule to a fact situation. I've many times had discussions with others in which we formulated rules together, seemed to agree about their terms, then engaged in a series of applications, finding that once we had agreed on the formula we would come up with the same answer to the question: how does the rule apply *here*?

I believe that it is possible to communicate with another person, so that we both have roughly the same rule in mind. I believe that it is possible to communicate with another so we both have roughly the same fact situation in mind. And I believe that when we both come up with the same answer to the question, "how does the rule apply to the facts?", it is sometimes meaningful to describe what has happened as "we applied the rule to the facts." In the situation I most fear as a liberal-law-reforming judge, when I have studied the various rules that I think might apply to the lie-in, I conclude that everyone will agree that the employer has a right to an injunction under the rules as we all understand them to be as of now, and that to change this particular rule would be unconstitutional. This conviction might be based on an "identical" case decided by the U.S. Supreme Court yesterday, or it might be based on a rather long and abstract chain of reasoning by analogy. But it might happen. And if it happened I would face some pretty tough choices about what to do in the case.

As I said, this declaration of faith in the possibility of communication and in the at least occasional intelligibility of the procedure of rule application doesn't meet your fancy argument on its own ground. I have no idea *why* this stuff happens. As I see it, your fancy argument is that I can't show an "objective basis" or a rationale or an explanation of rule application that will prove that any particular application was "correct". Indeed, the notion of correctness, at least as we usually use the word, say in math or science or logic, just isn't applicable.

I can't, from my position inside the practice of legal argument, say anything one way or another about this fancy argument. I have no way of knowing, from inside the practice, why it is that the field will sometimes give way but sometimes refuse to budge at all. Maybe when that happens it's just that I didn't find the catch that releases the secret panel. Maybe my sense that we communicated the rule to one another, and then each "applied" it, and that that's where the result "came from", is a false sense, a hopeful or sentimental or, in this lie-in case, a paranoid interpretation of the random fact that we agreed on the outcome, rather than a reflection of a common experience. From inside the practice of argument, I just don't know.

I will be very irritated indeed if you turn around on me now and reveal that you were just using the fancy argument to make me concede the truth of some form of positivism or objectivism about law, or at least legal rules. It was a good trick, but I claim to have evaded it. I have been saying all along that legal argument is the process of creating the field of law through restatement, rather than rule application. Rule application is something that does happen, but it is *never* something that *has* to happen. It is an outcome as contingent, as arbitrary, from the point of view of jurisprudence, as that in which the field is gloriously manipulable.

We dealt above with a case in which my initial apprehension was that the law was clear against the workers, but I was able to undermine the perceived objectivity of the rule (at least in a preliminary way). That was just an example among many possible of how an initial apprehension of ruledness can dissolve. Sometimes I approach the field in an agnostic frame of mind, and just can't figure out what the rule is supposed to be; sometimes I can't decide whether the facts are such that the outcome specified by the rule is triggered or not. Sometimes it seems there are several possible answers to the question and I don't have any feeling about which is correct. Sometimes I'm initially quite sure what the rule is and how to apply it, but a conversation with another person who has reached a different set of conclusions leaves me feeling neither that I was "right", nor that she was "right", but rather that the rule was in fact hopelessly ambiguous or internally contradictory all along.

If you tell me that law is rules, or that there is always a right answer to a legal problem, I will answer with these cases in which my experience was that law was indeterminate, or that I gave it its determinate shape as a matter of my free ethical or political choice. It is true that when we are unselfconsciously applying rules together, we have an unselfconscious experience of social objectivity. We know what is going to happen next by mentally applying the rule as others will, and then they apply the rule and it comes out the way we thought it would. But this is not in fact objectivity, and it is *always* vulnerable to different kinds of disruption—intentional and accidental—that suddenly disappoint our expectations of consensus and make people question their own sanity and that of others. This vulnerability of the field, its plasticity, its instability, are just as essential to it as we experience it as its sporadic quality of resistance.

The rule may at any given moment appear objective, but at the next moment it may appear manipulable. It is not, *as I apprehend it from within the practice of legal argument*, essentially one thing or the other.

If this is what it is like to ask the nature of law from within the practice of legal argument, then the answer to the question must come from outside that practice. All over the United States and indeed all over the world there are professors of jurisprudence who think they possess professional knowledge of the nature of law. Where are they getting it from? For my own part, I think their answers to questions like those I have been addressing are just made up out of whole cloth to wile away the evening or get tenure or legitimate the status quo or make pretty patterns or scratch the itch of existential dread before the unknowableness of the most important things in life. Show me your ground before you pretend to be moving the earth.